TO JESUS WITH MARY

Scriptural Rosary with Meditations on the
Life and Ministry of Jesus

CHARLES MICHAEL

Gifted Books and Media

Copyright

Scripture quotations are taken from the Douay-Rheims 1899 American Edition (Public domain) and from Catholic Public Domain Version (Public domain)

Compiled by Charles Michael

Printed in the United States of America

Paperback ISBN: 978-1-947343-10-8

Published by Jayclad Publishing LLC
www.giftedbookstore.com

Table of Contents

How to Pray the Scriptural Rosary

1. Make the Sign of the Cross

2. Say the "Apostles' Creed"

3. Say the "Our Father"

4. Say three "Hail Marys" for Faith, Hope, and Charity

5. Say the "Glory Be"

6. Announce the First Mystery

7. Say the "Our Father"

8. Read the Scripture verse before each Hail Mary (ten verses and ten Hail Marys per decade)

9. Say the "Glory Be"

10. Say the "O My Jesus" prayer

11. Announce the Next Mystery; and repeat the above steps (7-10).

12. Say the closing prayers (Hail Holy Queen, etc.)

13. Make the "Sign of the Cross"

The Joyful Mysteries

Decade 1 (The Annunciation)
Our Father…

In the sixth month, the Angel Gabriel was sent by God, to a city of Galilee named Nazareth, to a virgin betrothed to a man whose name was Joseph, of the house of David; and the name of the virgin was Mary. (Luk 1:26-27)
Hail Mary…

Upon entering, the Angel said to her: "Hail, full of grace. The Lord is with you. Blessed are you among women." (Luk 1:28)
Hail Mary…

When she had heard this, she was disturbed by his words, and she considered what kind of greeting this might be. (Luk 1:29)
Hail Mary…

The Angel said to her: "Do not be afraid, Mary, for you have found favor with God." (Luk 1:30)
Hail Mary…

Behold, you shall conceive in your womb, and you shall bear a son, and you shall call his name Jesus. (Luk 1:31)
Hail Mary…

He will be great, and he will be called the Son of the Most High, and the Lord God will give him the throne of David his father. And he will reign in the house of Jacob for eternity. And his kingdom shall have no end. (Luk 1:32-33)
Hail Mary…

Mary said to the angel, "since I am a virgin, how, then, can this be?" (Luk 1:34)
Hail Mary…

The angel said to her, "The Holy Spirit shall come upon you, and the power of the most High will overshadow you." (Luk 1:35)
Hail Mary…

Therefore the child who shall be born will be holy and he shall be called the Son of God. (Luk 1:35)

Hail Mary...

Then Mary said: "Behold, I am the handmaid of the Lord. Let it be done to me according to your word." And the Angel departed from her. (Luk 1:38)
Hail Mary...

Glory Be...

Decade 2 (The Visitation)
Our Father...

In those days, Mary, rising up, traveled quickly into the hill country, to a city of Judah. And she entered into the house of Zechariah, and she greeted Elizabeth. (Luk 1:39-40)
Hail Mary...

As Elizabeth heard the greeting of Mary, the baby leaped in her womb, and Elizabeth was filled with the Holy Spirit. (Luk 1:41)
Hail Mary...

Elizabeth was filled with the Holy Spirit. And she cried out with a loud voice and said: "Blessed are you among women, and blessed is the fruit of your womb." (Luk 1:41-42)
Hail Mary...

Blessed are you who believed, for the things that were spoken to you by the Lord shall be accomplished. (Luk 1:45)
Hail Mary...

Mary said: "My soul magnifies the Lord." (Luk 1:46)
Hail Mary

My spirit leaps for joy in God my Savior. (Luk 1:47)
Hail Mary...

He has looked with favor on the humility of his handmaid. (Luk 1:48)
Hail Mary...

Behold, from this time, all generations shall call me blessed. (Luk 1:48)
Hail Mary...

He has stretched out his mighty arm and he has scattered the proud in the thoughts of their hearts. (Luk 1:51)
Hail Mary...

He has filled the hungry with good things, and the rich he has sent away empty. (Luk 1:53)
Hail Mary...

Glory Be...

Decade 3 (The Nativity of our Lord Jesus Christ)
Our Father...

While they were in Bethlehem, the time came for her to have her baby. (Luk 2:6)
Hail Mary...

She brought forth her firstborn son. And she wrapped him in swaddling clothes. (Luk 2:7)
Hail Mary...

She wrapped him in swaddling clothes and laid him in a manger, because there was no room for them at the inn. (Luk 2:7)
Hail Mary...

There were some shepherds living in that part of the country, keeping the night watches over their flock. An angel of the Lord stood by them, and the glory of God shone round them, and they were terribly afraid. (Luk 2:8-9)
Hail Mary...

The Angel said to them: "Do not be afraid. For, behold, I proclaim to you good news of great joy, which will be for all the people. (Luk 2:10)
Hail Mary...

For today a Savior has been born for you in the city of David: he is the Messiah, the Lord. (Luk 2:11)
Hail Mary...

Glory to God in the highest, and on earth peace to those whom he favors. (Luk 2:14)
Hail Mary...

After the angels departed from them into heaven, the shepherds said one to another, "Let us go over to Bethlehem, and let us see this thing that has taken place, which the Lord has told us." (Luk 2:15)
Hail Mary...

When Jesus had been born in Bethlehem of Judah, in the days of king Herod, behold, Magi from the east arrived in Jerusalem. (Matt 2:1)

Hail Mary...

Entering the home, they found the boy with his mother Mary. And so, falling prostrate, they adored him. And opening their treasures, they offered him gifts: gold, frankincense, and myrrh. (Matt 2:11)
Hail Mary...

Glory Be…

Decade 4 (The Presentation of our Lord)
Our Father…

When it was time for their purification, according to the law of Moses, they brought him to Jerusalem, to present him to the Lord. (Luk 2:22)
Hail Mary...

There was a man in Jerusalem, whose name was Simeon, and this man was righteous and God-fearing, awaiting the consolation of Israel. And the Holy Spirit was upon him. (Luk 2:25)
Hail Mary...

The Holy Spirit was with him and had assured him that he would not die before he had seen the Lord's promised Messiah. (Luk 2:25-26)
Hail Mary...

He went to the temple, guided by the Holy Spirit. And when the child Jesus was brought in by his parents, in order to do for him according to the custom of the law, Simeon took him up, into his arms, and he praised God. (Luk 2:27-28)
Hail Mary...

Now you may dismiss your servant in peace, O Lord, according to your word. (Luk 2:29)
Hail Mary...

My eyes have seen your salvation, which you have prepared before the face of all peoples. (Luk 2:30-31)
Hail Mary...

The light of revelation to the nations and the glory of your people Israel. (Luk 2:32)
Hail Mary...

Simeon blessed them, and said to Mary his mother: Behold this child is destined for the fall, and for the rise of many in Israel, and to be a sign which will be contradicted. (Luk 2:34)

Hail Mary...

After they had performed all things according to the law of the Lord, they returned to Galilee, to their city, Nazareth. (Luk 2:39)
Hail Mary...

The child grew, and he was strengthened with the fullness of wisdom. And the grace of God was in him. (Luk 2:40)
Hail Mary...

Glory Be...

Decade 5 (The Finding of the Child Jesus in the Temple)
Our Father...

His parents went every year to Jerusalem, for the solemn festival of the Passover, and when Jesus was twelve years old, they went to the festival as usual. (Luk 2:41-42)
Hail Mary...

After the festival, they started back home, but the child Jesus remained in Jerusalem; and his parents did not know this. (Luk 2:43)
Hail Mary...

Thinking that he was in the group, they travelled a whole day's journey, and then started searching for him among their relatives and friends. And not finding him, they returned to Jerusalem, searching for him. (Luk 2:44-45)
Hail Mary...

After three days, they found him in the temple, sitting in the midst of the teachers, listening to them and asking them questions. (Luk 2:46)
Hail Mary...

All who listened to him were astonished over his prudence and his responses. (Luk 2:47)
Hail Mary...

Upon seeing him, they wondered. And his mother said to him: "Son, why have you acted this way toward us? Behold, your father and I were seeking you in sorrow." (Luk 2:48)
Hail Mary...

He said to them, "Why did you search for me? did you not know that I must be in my father's house?" (Luk 2:49)
Hail Mary...

They did not understand the word that he spoke to them. (Luk 2:50)
Hail Mary...

He went with them and came to Nazareth. And he was obedient to them. And his mother kept all these things in her heart. (Luk 2:51)
Hail Mary...

Jesus advanced in wisdom, and in age, and in grace, with God and men. (Luk 2:52)
Hail Mary...

Glory Be…

The Sorrowful Mysteries

Decade 1 (The Agony in the Garden)
Our Father...

Then Jesus went with them to a garden, which is called Gethsemane. And he said to his disciples, "Sit down here, while I go there and pray." (Matt 26:36)
Hail Mary...

Taking with him Peter and the two sons of Zebedee, he began to be sorrowful and saddened. (Matt 26:37)
Hail Mary...

Then he said to them: "My soul is sorrowful, even unto death. Stay here and keep vigil with me." (Matt 26:38)
Hail Mary...

Continuing on a little further, he fell prostrate on his face, praying and saying: "My Father, if it is possible, let this chalice pass away from me. Yet truly, let it not be as I will, but as you will." (Matt 26:39)
Hail Mary...

Again, a second time, he went and prayed, saying, "My Father, if this chalice cannot pass away, unless I drink it, let your will be done." (Matt 26:42)
Hail Mary...

And again, he went and found them sleeping, for their eyes were heavy. (Matt 26:43)
Hail Mary...

Leaving them behind, again he went and prayed for the third time, saying the same words. (Matt 26:44)
Hail Mary...

Then he approached his disciples and said to them: "Sleep now and rest. Behold, the hour has drawn near, and the Son of man will be delivered into the hands of sinners." (Matt 26:45)
Hail Mary...

Rise up; let us go. Behold, he who will betray me draws near. (Matt 26:46)
Hail Mary...

While he was still speaking, behold, Judas, one of the twelve, arrived, and with him was a large crowd with swords and clubs, sent from the leaders of the priests and the elders of the people. (Matt 26:47)
Hail Mary...

Glory Be...

Decade 2 (The Scourging at the Pillar)
Our Father...

Immediately in the morning, after the leaders of the priests had taken counsel with the elders and the scribes and the entire council, binding Jesus, they led him away and delivered him to Pilate. (Mrk 15:1-2)
Hail Mary...

Therefore, Pilate went outside to them, and he said, "What accusation are you bringing against this man?" (Jn 18:29)
Hail Mary...

They responded and said to him, "If he were not an evil-doer, we would not have handed him over to you." (Jn 18:30)
Hail Mary...

Therefore, Pilate said to them, "Take him yourselves and judge him according to your own law." Then the Jews said to him, "It is not lawful for us to execute anyone." (Jn 18:31)
Hail Mary...

Then Pilate entered the praetorium again, and he called Jesus and said to him, "You are the king of the Jews?" (Jn 18:33)
Hail Mary...

Jesus responded, "Are you saying this of yourself, or have others spoken to you about me?" (Jn 18:34)
Hail Mary...

Pilate responded: "Am I a Jew? Your own nation and the high priests have handed you over to me. What have you done?" (Jn 18:35)
Hail Mary...

Jesus responded: "My kingdom is not of this world. If my kingdom were of this world, my ministers would certainly strive so that I would not be handed over to the Jews. But my kingdom is not from here." (Jn 18:36-37)
Hail Mary...

Pilate said to him, "You are a king, then?" Jesus answered, "You are saying that I am a king. For this I was born, and for this I came into the world: so that I may offer testimony to the truth. Everyone who is of the truth hears my voice." Pilate said to him, "What is truth?" And when he had said this, he went out again to the Jews, and he said to them, "I find no case against him. (Jn 18:37-38)
Hail Mary...

Therefore, Pilate then took Jesus into custody and scourged him. (Jn 19:1)
Hail Mary...

Glory Be...

Decade 3 (The Crowning with the Thorns)
Our Father...

Then the soldiers led him away to the court of the praetorium. And they called together the entire cohort. (Mrk 15:16)
Hail Mary...

They clothed him with purple. And twisting a crown of thorns, they placed it on him. (Mrk 15:17)
Hail Mary...

And stripping him, they put a scarlet cloak around him. (Matt 27:28-29)
Hail Mary...

Plaiting a crown of thorns, they placed it on his head, with a reed in his right hand. And genuflecting before him, they mocked him, saying, "Hail, King of the Jews." (Matt 27:29)
Hail Mary...

And spitting on him, they took the reed and struck his head. (Matt 27:30)
Hail Mary...

And they began to salute him: "Hail, king of the Jews." (Mrk 15:18)
Hail Mary...

And they struck his head with a reed, and they spit on him. And kneeling down, they reverenced him. (Mrk 15:19)
Hail Mary...

Then Pilate went outside again, and he said to them: "Behold, I am bringing him out to you, so that you may realize that I find no case against him." (Then

Jesus went out, bearing the crown of thorns and the purple garment.) And he said to them, "Behold the man." (Jn 19:4-5)
Hail Mary...

But they were crying out: "Take him away! Take him away! Crucify him!" (Jn 19:15)
Hail Mary...

Pilate said to them, "Shall I crucify your king?" The high priests responded, "We have no king except Caesar."(Jn 19:15)
Hail Mary...

Glory Be...

Decade 4 (The Carrying of the Cross)
Our Father...

Therefore, he then handed him over to them to be crucified. And they took Jesus and led him away. (Jn 19:16)
Hail Mary...

After they had mocked him, they stripped him of the purple, and they clothed him in his own garments. And they led him away, so that they might crucify him. (Mrk 15:20)
Hail Mary...

Carrying his own cross, he went forth to the place, which is called Calvary, but in Hebrew it is called the Place of the Skull. (Jn 19:17)
Hail Mary...

They compelled a certain passerby, Simon the Cyrenian, who was arriving from the countryside, the father of Alexander and Rufus, to take up his cross. (Mrk 15:21)
Hail Mary...

Then a great crowd of people followed him, with women who were mourning and lamenting him. (Luk 23:27)
Hail Mary...

But Jesus, turning to them, said: "Daughters of Jerusalem, do not weep over me. Instead, weep over yourselves and over your children." (Luk 23:28)
Hail Mary...

For behold, the days will arrive in which they will say, 'Blessed are the barren, and the wombs that have not borne, and the breasts that have not nursed.' (Luk 23:29)
Hail Mary...

They led him through to the place called Golgotha, which means, 'the Place of Calvary.' And they gave him wine with myrrh to drink. But he did not accept it. (Mrk 15:22-23)
Hail Mary...

Then he said to everyone: "If anyone is willing to come after me: let him deny himself, and take up his cross every day, and follow me." (Luk 9:23)
Hail Mary...

For whoever will have saved his life, will lose it. Yet whoever will have lost his life for my sake, will save it. (Luk 9:24)
Hail Mary...

Glory Be…

Decade 5 (The Crucifixion)
Our Father…

When they arrived at the place that is called Calvary, they crucified him there, with the robbers, one to the right and the other to the left. (Luk 23:33)
Hail Mary...

Then Jesus said, "Father, forgive them. For they know not what they do." And truly, dividing his garments, they cast lots. (Luk 23:34)
Hail Mary...

The passersby blasphemed him, shaking their heads and saying, "Ah, you who would destroy the temple of God, and in three days rebuild it, save yourself by descending from the cross." (Mrk 15:29-30)
Hail Mary...

One of those robbers who were hanging blasphemed him, saying, "If you are the Christ, save yourself and us." (Luk 23:39)
Hail Mary...

But the other responded by rebuking him, saying: "Do you have no fear of God, since you are under the same condemnation?" (Luk 23:40)
Hail Mary...

Jesus said to him, "Amen I say to you, this day you shall be with me in Paradise." (Luk 23:43)
Hail Mary...

Standing beside the cross of Jesus were his mother, and his mother's sister, and Mary of Cleophas, and Mary Magdalene. Therefore, when Jesus had seen his mother and the disciple whom he loved standing near, he said to his mother, "Woman, behold your son." (Jn 19:25-26)
Hail Mary...

Now it was nearly the sixth hour, and a darkness occurred over the entire earth, until the ninth hour. (Luk 23:44)
Hail Mary...

Then Jesus, crying out again with a loud voice, gave up his life. (Matt 27:50)
Hail Mary...

Behold, the veil of the temple was torn into two parts, from top to bottom. And the earth was shaken, and the rocks were split apart. (Matt 27:51)
Hail Mary...

Glory Be

The Glorious Mysteries

Decade 1 (The Resurrection of our Lord)
Our Father…

Therefore, you also, indeed, have sorrow now. But I will see you again, and your heart shall rejoice. And no one will take away your joy from you. (Jn 16:22)
Hail Mary…

Then, on the first day of the week, early in the morning, they went to the tomb, carrying the aromatic spices that they had prepared. (Luk 24:1)
Hail Mary…

Behold, a great earthquake occurred. For an Angel of the Lord descended from heaven, and as he approached, he rolled back the stone and sat down on it. (Matt 28:2)
Hail Mary…

Then the Angel responded by saying to the women: "Do not be afraid. For I know that you are seeking Jesus, who was crucified. He is not here. For he has risen, just as he said. Come and see the place where the Lord was placed." (Matt 28:5-6)
Hail Mary…

He is not here, for he has risen. Recall how he spoke to you, when he was still in Galilee, saying: 'For the Son of man must be delivered into the hands of sinful men, and be crucified, and on the third day rise again.' (Luk 24:6-7)
Hail Mary…

Go quickly and tell his disciples that he has been raised from death: and behold he will go before you into Galilee; there you shall see him. Remember what I have told you. (Matt 28:7)
Hail Mary…

They went out of the tomb quickly, with fear and in great joy, running to announce it to his disciples. (Matt 28:8)
Hail Mary…

And Suddenly Jesus met them, saying, "Peace be with you." They came up and took hold of his feet, and worshiped him. (Matt 28:9)
Hail Mary…

Then Jesus said to them: "Do not be afraid. Go, announce it to my brothers, so that they may go to Galilee. There they shall see me." (Matt 28:10)
Hail Mary...

After his suffering, he also presented himself alive to them by many proofs, appearing to them throughout forty days and speaking about the kingdom of God. (Acts 1:3)
Hail Mary...

Glory Be...

Decade 2 (The Ascension)
Our Father...

Then he led them out as far as Bethania. And lifting up his hands, he blessed them. (Luk 24:50)
Hail Mary...

Jesus, drawing near, spoke to them, saying: "All authority has been given to me in heaven and on earth." (Matt 28:18)
Hail Mary...

Therefore, go forth and teach all nations, baptizing them in the name of the Father and of the Son and of the Holy Spirit. (Matt 28:19)
Hail Mary...

Teach them to observe all that I have ever commanded you. (Matt 28:20)
Hail Mary...

Behold, I am with you always, even to the end of the age. (Matt 28:20)
Hail Mary...

It happened that, while he was blessing them, he withdrew from them, and he was carried up into heaven. (Luk 24:51)
Hail Mary...

Indeed, the Lord Jesus, after he had spoken to them, was taken up into heaven, and he sits at the right hand of God. (Mrk 16:19)
Hail Mary...

They worshiped him and they returned to Jerusalem with great joy. (Luk 24:52)
Hail Mary...

They were always in the temple, praising and blessing God. (Luk 24:53)

Hail Mary...

They went forth, and preached the good news everywhere, the Lord worked with them, and confirmed the word with signs that accompanied it. (Mrk 16:20)
Hail Mary...

Glory Be…

Decade 3 (The Coming of the Holy Spirit)
Our Father…

I am sending the Promise of my Father upon you. But you must stay in the city, until such time as you are clothed with power from on high. (Luk 24:49)
Hail Mary...

When they were together, he commanded them, "Do not leave Jerusalem but wait for the promise of the Father, which you have heard from me. For John indeed baptized with water, but you shall be baptized with the Holy Spirit, not many days from now." (Acts 1:4-5)
Hail Mary...

When they had entered the city, they went upstairs to the room where Peter and John, James and Andrew, Philip and Thomas, Bartholomew and Matthew, James of Alphaeus and Simon the Zealot, and Jude of James, were staying. (Acts 1:13)
Hail Mary...

When the days of Pentecost were completed, they were all together in the same place. And suddenly, there came a sound from heaven, like that of a wind approaching violently, and it filled the entire house where they were sitting. (Acts 2:1-2)
Hail Mary...

There appeared to them divided tongues, as if of fire, and a tongue rested upon each one of them. (Acts 2:3)
Hail Mary...

They were all filled with the Holy Spirit, and they began to speak in other languages, as the Holy Spirit enabled them to speak. (Acts 2:4)
Hail Mary...

When this sound occurred, the multitude came together and was confused in mind, because each one was listening to them speaking in his own language. (Acts 2:6)

Hail Mary...

Therefore, being exalted to the right hand of God, and having received from the Father the Promise of the Holy Spirit, he poured this out, just as you now see and hear. (Acts 2:33)
Hail Mary...

I will pour out my spirit upon all flesh, and your sons and your daughters will prophesy; your elders will dream dreams, and your youths will see visions. (Joel 2:28)
Hail Mary...

In those days I will pour out my spirit upon my servants and handmaids. And I will grant wonders in the sky and on earth: blood and fire and the vapor of smoke. (Joel 2:29-30)
Hail Mary...

Glory Be...

Decade 4 (The Assumption of the Blessed Virgin Mary)
Our Father...

The temple of God was opened in heaven. And the Ark of his covenant was seen in his temple. And there were flashes of lightnings and noises, and thunders, and an earthquake, and great hail. (Rev 11:19)
Hail Mary...

Great sign appeared in heaven: a woman clothed with the sun, and the moon was under her feet, and on her head was a crown of twelve stars. (Rev 12:1)
Hail Mary...

She was about to give birth, she cried out while giving birth because of the pain and suffering of childbirth. (Rev 12:2)
Hail Mary...

After the dragon saw that he had been thrown down to the earth, he pursued the woman who brought forth the male child. (Rev 12:13)
Hail Mary...

The two wings of a great eagle were given to the woman, so that she might fly away from the serpent, into the wilderness, to her place, where she is nourished for a time, and times, and half a time. (Rev 12:14)
Hail Mary...

The dragon was angry at the woman. And so he went away to do battle with the remainder of her offspring, those who keep the commandments of God and who hold to the testimony of Jesus Christ. (Rev 12:17)
Hail Mary...

The prayer of one who humbles himself will pierce the clouds. And it will not be consoled until it reaches its goal; and it will not withdraw until the Most High beholds. (Sir 35:21)
Hail Mary...

Be humbled under the powerful hand of God, so that he may exalt you in the time of visitation. (1 Pet 5:6)
Hail Mary...

God resists the proud, but gives grace to the humble. (Jas 4:6)
Hail Mary...

Seek the Lord, all you meek of the earth, who obey his commands. seek righteousness, seek humility: if may be that you may be hidden on the day of the Lord's anger. (Zeph 2:3)
Hail Mary...

Glory Be...

Decade 5 (The Coronation of the Blessed Mother)
Our Father...

He who is mighty has done great things for me, and holy is his name. (Luk 1:49)
Hail Mary...

The Lord has blessed you more than any other woman on earth. Blessed be the Lord who made heaven and earth. (Judith 13:18, Judith 13:23-24)
Hail Mary...

All these were constantly devoting themselves in prayer with the women, including Mary, the mother of Jesus, and with his brothers. (Acts 1:14)
Hail Mary...

Through the heart of the mercy of our God, by which, descending from on high, he has visited us, to illuminate those who sit in darkness and in the shadow of death, and to direct our feet in the way of peace. (Luk 1:78-79)
Hail Mary...

It happened that, when he was saying these things, a certain woman from the crowd, lifting up her voice, said to him, "Blessed is the womb that bore you and the breasts that nursed you." (Luk 11:27)
Hail Mary...

My song will cause your name to be celebrated throughout all generations. Everyone will praise you forever. (Ps 45:17, Ps 44:18)
Hail Mary...

When Jesus had seen his mother and the disciple whom he loved standing near, he said to his mother, "Woman, behold your son." Next, he said to the disciple, "Behold your mother." And from that hour, the disciple accepted her as his own. (Jn 19:26-27)
Hail Mary...

Obedience is better than sacrifice. And to heed is greater than to offer the fat of rams. (1 Sam 15:22)
Hail Mary...

Blessed are those who preserve my ways. Listen to discipline, and become wise, and do not be willing to cast it aside. (Pro 8:32-33)
Hail Mary...

Whoever listens to me will not be put to shame, and whoever works with me will not sin. (Sir 24:22)
Hail Mary...

Glory Be...

The Luminous Mysteries

Decade 1 (The Baptism of our Lord)
Our Father…

I baptize you with water for repentance, but he who will come after me is more powerful than me. I am not worthy to carry his shoes. He will baptize you with the fire of the Holy Spirit. (Matt 3:11)
Hail Mary…

This is the one about whom I said, "After me comes a man, who is greater than me, because he was before me." (Jn 1:30)
Hail Mary…

I myself did not know him. Yet it is for this reason that I come baptizing with water: so that he may be revealed to Israel. (Jn 1:31)
Hail Mary…

Jesus came from Galilee, to John at the Jordan, in order to be baptized by him. (Matt 3:13)
Hail Mary…

John tried to prevent him, saying, "I ought to be baptized by you, yet you have come to me." (Matt 3:14)
Hail Mary…

Jesus answering, said to him, "Let it to be so for now. For in this way, we shall fulfill all righteousness. Then John agreed. (Matt 3:15)
Hail Mary…

Jesus, having been baptized, ascended from the water immediately, and behold, the heavens were opened to him. And he saw the Spirit of God descending like a dove, and alighting on him. (Matt 3:16)
Hail Mary…

Behold, there was a voice from heaven, saying: "This is my beloved Son, in whom I am well pleased." (Matt 3:17)
Hail Mary…

John offered testimony, saying: "For I saw the Spirit descending from heaven like a dove; and he remained upon him." (Jn 1:32)
Hail Mary…

I did not know him. But he who sent me to baptize with water said to me: 'He over whom you will see the Spirit descending and remaining upon him, this is the one who baptizes with the Holy Spirit.' (Jn 1:33)
Hail Mary...

Glory Be...

Decade 2 (The Wedding at Cana)
Our Father...

On the third day, a wedding was held in Cana of Galilee, and the mother of Jesus was there. Now Jesus was also invited to the wedding, with his disciples. (Jn 2:1-2)
Hail Mary...

And when the wine had given out, the mother of Jesus said to him, "They have no wine." (Jn 2:3)
Hail Mary...

Jesus said to her: "What is that to me and to you, woman? My hour has not yet arrived." (Jn 2:4)
Hail Mary...

His mother said to the servants, "Do whatever he tells you." (Jn 2:5)
Hail Mary...

Now in that place, there were six stone water jars, for the purification ritual of the Jews, each holding twenty or thirty gallons. (Jn 2:6)
Hail Mary...

Jesus said to them, "Fill the water jars with water." And they filled them to the very top. (Jn 2:7)
Hail Mary...

Jesus said to them, "Now draw from it, and carry it to the chief steward of the feast." And they took it to him. (Jn 2:8)
Hail Mary...

When the chief steward had tasted the water made into wine, since he did not know where it was from, for only the servants who had drawn the water knew, the chief steward called the groom. (Jn 2:9)
Hail Mary...

He said to him: "Everyone offers the good wine first, and then, when they have become drunk, they offer what is inferior. But you have kept the good wine until now." (Jn 2:10)
Hail Mary...

This was the beginning of the signs that Jesus accomplished in Cana of Galilee, and it manifested his glory, and his disciples believed in him. (Jn 2:11)
Hail Mary...

Glory Be…

Decade 3 (The Proclamation of the Kingdom)
Our Father…

The time has been fulfilled and the kingdom of God has drawn near. Repent and believe in the Gospel. (Mrk 1:15)
Hail Mary...

Jesus responded: "Amen, amen, I say to you, unless one has been reborn by water and the Holy Spirit, he is not able to enter into the kingdom of God." (Jn 3:5)
Hail Mary...

From that time, Jesus began to preach, and to say: "Repent. For the kingdom of heaven has drawn near." (Matt 4:17)
Hail Mary...

Jesus traveled throughout all of Galilee, teaching in their synagogues, and preaching the Gospel of the kingdom, and healing every sickness and every infirmity among the people. (Matt 4:23)
Hail Mary...

Going forth, preach, saying: 'For the kingdom of heaven has drawn near.' Cure the infirm, raise the dead, cleanse lepers, cast out demons. You have received freely, so give freely. (Matt 10:7-8)
Hail Mary...

Into whatever city you have entered and they have received you, eat what they set before you. And cure the sick who are in that place, and proclaim to them, 'The kingdom of God has drawn near to you.' (Luk 10:8-9)
Hail Mary...

This good news of the kingdom shall be preached throughout the entire world, as a testimony to all nations. And then the end will occur. (Matt 24:14)

Hail Mary...

It happened afterwards that he was making a journey through the cities and towns, preaching and evangelizing the kingdom of God. And the twelve were with him. (Luk 8:1)
Hail Mary...

When the crowd had realized this, they followed him. And he received them and spoke to them about the kingdom of God. And those who were in need of cures, he healed. (Luk 9:11)
Hail Mary...

Jesus traveled throughout all of the cities and towns, teaching in their synagogues, and preaching the Gospel of the kingdom, and healing every illness and every infirmity. (Matt 9:35)
Hail Mary...

Glory Be...

Decade 4 (The Transfiguration)
Our Father...

After six days, Jesus took Peter and James and his brother John, and he led them onto a lofty mountain separately. (Matt 17:1)
Hail Mary...

He was transfigured before them. And his face shined brightly like the sun. And his garments were made white like snow. (Matt 17:2)
Hail Mary...

Behold, there appeared to them Moses and Elijah, speaking with him. (Matt 17:3)
Hail Mary...

His vestments became radiant and exceedingly white like snow, such as no one on earth is able to whiten them. (Mrk 9:3)
Hail Mary...

Peter responded by saying to Jesus: "Lord, it is good for us to be here. If you are willing, let us make three tabernacles here, one for you, one for Moses, and one for Elijah." (Matt 17:4)
Hail Mary...

While he was still speaking, behold, a shining cloud overshadowed them. And behold, there was a voice from the cloud, saying: "This is my beloved Son, with whom I am well pleased. Listen to him." (Matt 17:5)
Hail Mary...

The disciples, when they heard the voice, they fell on their faces and were very afraid. (Matt 17:6)
Hail Mary...

Jesus drew near and touched them. And he said to them, "Rise up and do not be afraid." (Matt 17:7)
Hail Mary...

Lifting up their eyes, they saw no one, except Jesus alone. (Matt 17:8)
Hail Mary...

As they were descending from the mountain, Jesus instructed them, saying, "Tell no one about the vision, until the Son of man has risen from the dead." (Matt 17:9)
Hail Mary...

Glory Be…

Decade 5 (The Institution of the Last Supper)
Our Father…

On the first day of Unleavened Bread, the disciples approached Jesus, saying, "Where do you want us to prepare for you to eat the Passover?" (Matt 26:17)
Hail Mary...

Jesus said, "Go into the city, to a certain one, and say to him: 'The Teacher said: My time is near. I am observing the Passover with you, along with my disciples.' "(Matt 26:18)
Hail Mary...

The disciples did just as Jesus appointed to them. And they prepared the Passover. (Matt 26:19)
Hail Mary...

When evening arrived, he sat at table with his twelve disciples. And while they were eating, he said: "Amen I say to you, that one of you is about to betray me." (Matt 26:20-21)
Hail Mary...

Being greatly saddened, each one of them began to say, "Surely, it is not I, Lord?" But he responded by saying: "The one who dips his hand into the bowl with me will betray me. (Matt 26:22-23)
Hail Mary...

Indeed, the Son of man goes, just as it has been written about him. But woe to that man by whom the Son of man will be betrayed. It would be better for that man if he had not been born. (Matt 26:24)
Hail Mary...

While they were eating the meal, Jesus took bread, and he blessed and broke and gave it to his disciples, and he said: "Take and eat. This is my body." (Matt 26:26)
Hail Mary...

Taking the chalice, he gave thanks. And he gave it to them, saying: "Drink from this, all of you." (Matt 26:27)
Hail Mary...

This is my blood of the new covenant, which shall be shed for many for the forgiveness of sins. (Matt 26:28)
Hail Mary...

But I say to you, I will not drink again from this fruit of the vine, until that day when I will drink it new with you in the kingdom of my Father. (Matt 26:29)
Hail Mary...

Glory Be...

Jesus, the Suffering Servant

Scriptural Rosary based on Jesus' call to suffer for the sins of humankind

---

Decade 1
Our Father...

Isaac said to his father Abraham, "Father". And he answered, "yes, my son? "Behold, the fire and the wood are here," he said, "but where is the lamb for the sacrifice?" And Abraham said, "My son, God will himself provide the lamb for the sacrifice." (Gen 22:7-8)
Hail Mary...

My God, my God, why have you forsaken me? why are you so far from helping me, and from the words of my groaning? (Ps 22:1/ Ps 21:2)
Hail Mary...

All those who trouble me are in your sight; my heart has anticipated reproach and misery. And I sought for one who might grieve together with me, but there was no one, and for one who might console me, and I found no one. And they gave me gall for my food. And in my thirst, they gave me vinegar to drink. (Ps 68:21-22)
Hail Mary...

Just as they were astonished over you, so will his countenance be without glory among men, and his appearance, among mortals. (Is 52:14)
Hail Mary...

He will rise up like a tender plant in his sight, and like a root from the thirsty ground. There is no beautiful or stately appearance in him. For we looked upon him, and there was no aspect, such that we would desire him. (Is 53:2)
Hail Mary...

He is despised and the least among men, a man of sorrows who knows infirmity. And his countenance was hidden and despised. Because of this, we did not esteem him. (Is 53:3)
Hail Mary...

Truly, he has taken away our weaknesses, and he himself has carried our sorrows. And we thought of him as if he were a leper, or as if he had been struck by God and humiliated. (Is 53:4)
Hail Mary...

He himself was wounded because of our iniquities. He was bruised because of our wickedness. The discipline of our peace was upon him. And by his wounds, we are healed. (Is 53:5)
Hail Mary...

We have all gone astray like sheep; each one has turned aside to his own way. And the Lord has placed all our iniquity upon him. (Is 53:6)
Hail Mary...

He was offered up, because it was his own will. And he did not open his mouth. He will be led like a sheep to the slaughter. And he will be mute like a lamb before his shearer. For he will not open his mouth. (Is 53:7)
Hail Mary...

Glory Be...

Decade 2
Our Father...

He was lifted up from anguish and judgment. Who will describe his life? For he has been cut off from the land of the living. Because of the wickedness of my people, I have struck him down. (Is 53:8)
Hail Mary...

He will be given a place with the impious for his burial, and with the rich for his death, though he has done no iniquity, nor was deceit in his mouth. (Is 53:9)
Hail Mary...

It was the will of the Lord to crush him with infirmity. If he lays down his life because of sin, he will see offspring with long lives, and the will of the Lord will be directed by his hand. (Is 53:10)
Hail Mary...

Because his soul has labored, he will see and be satisfied. By his knowledge, my just servant will himself justify many, and he himself will carry their iniquities. (Is 53:11)
Hail Mary...

Therefore, I will allot to him a great number. And he will divide the spoils of the strong. For he has handed over his life to death, and he was reputed among criminals. And he has taken away the sins of many, and he has prayed for the transgressors. (Is 53:12)
Hail Mary…

From that time Jesus began to show his disciples that he must go to Jerusalem, and suffer many things from the elders, the scribes, and the chief priests, and be put to death, and on the third day rise again. (Matt 16:21)
Hail Mary…

Behold, we are ascending to Jerusalem, and the Son of man shall be handed over to the leaders of the priests and to the scribes. And they shall condemn him to death. And they shall hand him over to the Gentiles to be mocked and scourged and crucified. And on the third day, he shall rise again. (Matt 20:18-19)
Hail Mary…

And many, upon hearing him, were amazed at his teaching, saying: "Where did this one get all these things?" and, "What is this wisdom, which has been given to him?" and, "Such powerful deeds, which are done by his hands! Is this not the carpenter, the son of Mary, the brother of James, and Joseph, and Jude, and Simon? Are not his sisters also here with us?" And they took great offense at him. (Mrk 6:2-3)
Hail Mary…

He began to teach them, that the Son of Man must suffer many things, and be rejected by the elders and by the chief priests, and the scribes, and be killed, and after three days rise again. (Mrk 8:31)
Hail Mary…

Behold, we are going up to Jerusalem, and the Son of man will be handed over to the leaders of the priests, and to the scribes, and the elders. And they will condemn him to death, and they will hand him over to the Gentiles. And they will mock him, and spit on him, and scourge him, and put him to death. (Mrk 10:33-34)
Hail Mary…

Glory Be…

Decade 3
Our Father…

They said, "Grant to us that we may sit, one at your right and the other at your left, in your glory." But Jesus said to them: "You do not know what you

are asking. Are you able to drink from the chalice from which I drink, or to be baptized with the baptism with which I am to be baptized?" (Mrk 10:37-38)
Hail Mary…

All those in the synagogue, upon hearing these things, were filled with anger. And they rose up and drove him beyond the city. And they brought him all the way to the edge of the mount, upon which their city had been built, so that they might throw him down violently. (Luk 4:28-29)
Hail Mary…

For just as lightning flashes from under heaven and shines to whatever is under heaven, so also will the Son of man be in his day. But first he must suffer many things and be rejected by this generation. (Luk 17:24-25)
Hail Mary…

Then Jesus took the twelve aside, and he said to them: "Behold, we are ascending to Jerusalem, and everything shall be completed which was written by the prophets about the Son of man. For he will be handed over to the Gentiles, and he will be mocked and scourged and spit upon. And after they have scourged him, they will kill him. (Luk 18:31-33)
Hail Mary…

The lord of the vineyard said: 'What shall I do? I will send my beloved son. Perhaps when they have seen him, they will respect him.' And when the tenants had seen him, they discussed it among themselves, saying: 'This one is the heir. Let us kill him, so that the inheritance will be ours.' And forcing him outside of the vineyard, they killed him. (Luk 20:13-15)
Hail Mary…

He was separated from them by about a stone's throw. And kneeling down, he prayed, saying: "Father, if you are willing, take this chalice away from me. Yet truly, let not my will, but yours, be done." (Luk 22:42-44)
Hail Mary…

He said to them: "How foolish and reluctant in heart you are, to believe everything that has been spoken by the Prophets! Was not the Christ required to suffer these things, and then enter into his glory?" (Luk 24:25-26)
Hail Mary…

Then he opened their minds, that they might understand the scriptures. And he said to them, "Thus it is written, that it was necessary for the Messiah to suffer, and to rise again from the dead on the third day. (Luk 24:45-46)
Hail Mary…

He was in the world, and the world was made through him, and the world did not recognize him. He went to his own, and his own did not accept him. (Jn 1:10-11)
Hail Mary…

Just as Moses lifted up the serpent in the desert, so also must the Son of man be lifted up, so that whoever believes in him may not perish, but may have eternal life. (Jn 3:14-15)
Hail Mary…

Glory Be…

Decade 4
Our Father…

Jesus said to Peter: "Set your sword into its sheath. Should I not drink the chalice which my Father has given to me?" (Jn 18:11)
Hail Mary…

Then Paul, according to custom, entered to them. And for three Sabbaths he disputed with them about the Scriptures, interpreting and concluding that it was necessary for the Christ to suffer and to rise again from the dead, and that "This is the Jesus Christ, whom I am announcing to you." (Acts 17:2-3)
Hail Mary…

For God made him who did not know sin to be sin for us, so that we might become the justice of God in him. (2 Cor 5:21)
Hail Mary…

Christ has redeemed us from the curse of the law, since he became a curse for us. For it is written: "Cursed is anyone who hangs from a tree." (Gal 3:13)
Hail Mary…

We understand that Jesus, who was reduced to a little less than the Angels, was crowned with glory and honor because of his passion and death, in order that, by the grace of God, he might taste death for all. (Heb 2:9)
Hail Mary…

It was fitting for God, for whom are all things, and by whom are all things, who had brought many children into glory, to make the author of their salvation, perfect through sufferings. (Heb 2:10)
Hail Mary…

It is Christ who, in the days of his flesh, with a strong cry and tears, offered prayers and supplications to the One who was able to save him from death,

and who was heard because of his reverence. And although, certainly, he is the Son of God, he learned obedience by the things that he suffered. (Heb 5:7-8)
Hail Mary…

Let us gaze upon Jesus, as the Author and perfecter of our faith, who, having joy laid out before him, endured the cross, disregarding the shame, and who now sits at the right hand of the throne of God. (Heb 12:2)
Hail Mary…

So then, meditate upon him who endured such adversity from sinners against himself, so that you may not become weary, failing in your souls. (Heb 12:3)
Hail Mary…

You have been called to this because Christ also suffered for us, leaving you an example, so that you would follow in his footsteps. He committed no sin, neither was deceit found in his mouth. (1 Pet 2:21-22)
Hail Mary…

Glory Be…

Decade 5
Our Father…

When he was reviled, he did not revile back: when he suffered, he did not threaten; but placed his hope in God who judges righteously. (1 Pet 2:23)
Hail Mary…

He himself bore our sins in his body upon the tree, so that we, having died to sin, would live for justice. By his wounds, you have been healed. (1 Pet 2:24)
Hail Mary…

It is better to suffer for doing good, if it is the will of God, than for doing evil. For Christ also died once for our sins, the Just One on behalf of the unjust, so that he might offer us to God, having died, certainly, in the flesh, but having been enlivened by the Spirit. (1 Pet 3:17-18)
Hail Mary…

The leaders of the priests, mocking him with the scribes, said to one another: "He saved others. He is not able to save himself. Let the Christ, the king of Israel, descend now from the cross, so that we may see and believe." Those who were crucified with him also insulted him. (Mrk 15:31-32)
Hail Mary…

I have given my body to those who strike me, and my cheeks to those who plucked them. I have not averted my face from those who rebuked me and who spit on me. (Is 50:6)
Hail Mary…

I am poured out like water; and all my bones are scattered. My heart is become like wax melting within me. My strength is dried up like a potsherd, and my tongue has cleaved to my jaws; and you have brought me to the dust of death. (Ps 22:14-15, Ps 21:15-16)
Hail Mary…

For many dogs have encompassed me: a company of evildoers have encircled me. They have dug my hands and feet. I can count my bones. And they have looked and stared upon me. (Ps 22:16-17, Ps 21:17-18)
Hail Mary…

I will pour out upon the house of David and upon the inhabitants of Jerusalem, the spirit of grace and of prayers. And they will look upon me, whom they have pierced, and they will mourn for Him as one mourns for an only son, and they will feel sorrow over him, as one would be sorrowful at the death of a firstborn. (Zech 12:10)
Hail Mary…

Come to the Lord, a living stone rejected by people, but chosen and honored by God. (1 Pet 2:4)
Hail Mary…

He humbled himself, becoming obedient even unto death, even the death of the Cross. (Phil 2:8)
Hail Mary…

Glory Be…

Prophecies about Jesus I

Decade 1
Our Father…

The scepter from Judah shall not depart, nor the leader's staff from between his feet will be taken away, until he who will be sent arrives, and to him shall be the obedience of the people. (Gen 49:10)
Hail Mary…

When your days will have been fulfilled, and you will sleep with your fathers, I will raise up your offspring after you, who will go forth from your loins, and I will make firm his kingdom. He himself shall build a house to my name. And I will establish the throne of his kingdom forever. (2 Sam 7:12-13)
Hail Mary…

The Lord himself will grant to you a sign. Behold, a virgin will conceive, and she will give birth to a son, and his name will be called Immanuel. (Is 7:14)
Hail Mary…

Israel was a child and I loved him; and out of Egypt I called my son. (Hos 11:1)
Hail Mary…

You, Bethlehem of Ephrathah, are a little one among the thousands of Judah. From you will go forth he who shall be the ruler in Israel, and his origin has been set from the beginning, from the days of eternity. (Mic 5:2)
Hail Mary…

I will put enmity between you and the woman, and your offspring and her offspring: he shall strike your head, and you shall strike his heel. (Gen 3:15)
Hail Mary…

I will open my mouth in parables: I will utter things from of old. (Ps 78:2, Ps 77:2)
Hail Mary…

He shall be a sanctuary to you. He will be a stone of stumbling and a rock of offence to the two houses of Israel, and a snare and a ruin to the inhabitants of Jerusalem. (Is 8:14)
Hail Mary…

In the earlier time, the land of Zebulun and the land of Naphtali were lifted up. But in the later time, the way of the sea beyond the Jordan, the Galilee of the Gentiles, was weighed down. The people who walked in darkness have seen a great light. A light has risen for the inhabitants of the region of the shadow of death. (Is 9:1-2)
Hail Mary...

A child is born to us, and a son is given to us, upon his shoulder dominion rests, and his name shall be called, Wonderful Counsellor, Mighty God, Eternal Father, Prince of Peace. (Is 9:6)
Hail Mary...

Glory Be...

Decade 2
Our Father...

In that day, the root of Jesse, who stands as a sign among the people, the nations shall inquire of him, and his sepulcher will be glorious. (Is 11:10)
Hail Mary...

There shall come forth a shoot out of the stump of Jesse, and a branch shall rise up out of his root. (Is 11:1)
Hail Mary...

Strengthen the weak hands and make firm the weak knees. Say to the fainthearted: Take courage, and fear not: behold your God will come with the revenge of recompense: God himself will come and will save you. (Is 35:3-4)
Hail Mary...

The voice of one crying out in the desert: "Prepare the way of the Lord! Make straight the paths of our God, in a solitary place. Every valley will be exalted, and every mountain and hill will be brought low. And the crooked will be straightened, and the uneven will become level ways." (Is 40:3-4)
Hail Mary...

Behold my servant, I will uphold him, my elect, with him my soul is well-pleased. I have sent my Spirit upon him. He will offer judgment to the nations. He will not cry out, and he will not show favoritism to anyone; neither will his voice be heard abroad. The bruised reed he will not break, and the smoldering wick he will not extinguish. He will lead forth judgment unto truth. He will not be saddened or troubled, until he establishes judgment on earth. (Is 42:1-4)
Hail Mary...

He will rise up like a tender plant in his sight, and like a root from the thirsty ground. There is no beautiful or stately appearance in him. For we looked upon him, and there was no aspect, such that we would desire him. (Is 53:2)
Hail Mary...

He is despised and the least among men, a man of sorrows who knows infirmity. And his countenance was hidden and despised. Because of this, we did not esteem him. (Is 53:3)
Hail Mary...

Surely he has borne our infirmities and carried our sorrows: and we thought of him as stricken, and as one smitten by God and afflicted. (Is 53:4)
Hail Mary...

He himself was wounded because of our iniquities. He was bruised because of our wickedness. The discipline of our peace was upon him. And by his wounds, we are healed. (Is 53:5)
Hail Mary...

We have all gone astray like sheep; each one has turned aside to his own way. And the Lord has placed all our iniquity upon him. (Is 53:6)
Hail Mary...

Glory Be...

Decade 3
Our Father...

He was oppressed, and he was afflicted, yet he did not open his mouth. He is led as a lamb to the slaughter and silent as a sheep before his shearer, and he did not open his mouth. (Is 53:7)
Hail Mary...

I watched, therefore, in the vision of the night, and behold, with the clouds of heaven, one like a son of man arrived, and he approached all the way to the Ancient of days, and they presented him before him. And he gave him power, and honor, and the kingdom, and all peoples, tribes, and languages will serve him. His power is an eternal power, which will not be taken away, and his kingdom, one which will not be corrupted. (Dan 7:13-14)
Hail Mary...

Rejoice well, daughter of Zion, shout for joy, daughter of Jerusalem. Behold, your King will come to you: the Just One, the Savior. He is poor and riding upon a donkey, and upon a colt, the son of a donkey. (Zech 9:9)
Hail Mary...

They weighed for my wages thirty silver coins. And the Lord said to me: Cast it towards the treasury, the handsome price at which I have been valued by them. And I took the thirty silver coins, and I cast them into the house of the Lord, towards the treasury. (Zech 11:12-13)
Hail Mary...

Behold, I will send to you Elijah the prophet, before the arrival of the great and terrible day of the Lord. And he will turn the heart of the parents to the children, and the heart of the children to their parents. (Mal 4:5-6)
Hail Mary...

The life of the flesh is in the blood, and I have given it to you, so that you may atone with it upon the altar for your souls, and so that the blood may be for an expiation of the soul. (Lev 17:11)
Hail Mary...

I know that my Redeemer lives, and that he will, at the last, stand upon the earth. (Job 19:25)
Hail Mary...

My God, my God, why have you forsaken me? why are you so far from helping me, and from the words of my groaning? (Ps 22:1, Ps 21:2)
Hail Mary...

My strength is dried up like a potsherd, and my tongue has cleaved to my jaws; and you have brought me to the dust of death. (Ps 22:15, Ps 21:16)
Hail Mary...

For many dogs have encompassed me: a company of evildoers have encircled me. They have dug my hands and feet. I can count my bones. And they have looked and stared upon me. (Ps 22:16-17, Ps 21:17-18)
Hail Mary...

Glory Be…

Decade 4
Our Father…

They divided my garments amongst themselves; and for my clothing they cast lots. (Ps 22:18/ Ps 21:19)
Hail Mary...

Into your hands I commit my spirit: you have redeemed me, O Lord, faithful God. (Ps 31:5/ Ps 30:5)
Hail Mary...

I have become a reproach among all my enemies, and especially my neighbors. Those who know me are afraid of me. When they see me, they flee from me. (Ps 31:11)
Hail Mary...

I have heard the blame of many, terror is all around me. While they assembled against me, they plot to take away my life. (Ps 30:14/ Ps 31:13)
Hail Mary...

I looked for one that would grieve together with me, but there was none: and for one that would comfort me, and I found none. And they gave me gall for my food, and in my thirst, they gave me vinegar to drink. (Ps 69:20-21, Ps 68:21-22)
Hail Mary...

I shall not die, but live: and shall declare the works of the Lord. (Ps 118:17, Ps 117:17)
Hail Mary...

I will place the key of the house of David upon his shoulder. And when he opens, no one will close. And when he closes, no one will open. And I will fasten him like a peg in a trustworthy place. And he will be upon a throne of glory in the house of his father. (Is 22:22-23)
Hail Mary...

He said to them: "How foolish and reluctant in heart you are, to believe everything that has been spoken by the Prophets! Was not the Christ required to suffer these things, and so enter into his glory?" And beginning from Moses and all the Prophets, he interpreted for them, in all the Scriptures, the things that were about him. (Luk 24:25-27)
Hail Mary...

I will strike a covenant of peace with them. This will be an everlasting covenant for them. And I will establish them, and multiply them. And I will set my sanctuary in their midst, unceasingly. And my tabernacle shall be among them. And I will be their God, and they will be my people. (Eze 37:26-27)
Hail Mary...

I will allot to him a great number. And he will divide the spoils of the strong. For he has handed over his life to death, and he was reputed among criminals. And he has taken away the sins of many, and he has prayed for the transgressors. (Is 53:12)
Hail Mary...

Glory Be…

Decade 5
Our Father…

Behold, I will set a stone within the foundations of Zion, a tested stone, a cornerstone, a precious stone, which has been established in the foundation: whoever trusts in him will not panic. (Is 28:16)
Hail Mary…

I have given my body to those who strike me, and my cheeks to those who plucked them. I have not averted my face from those who rebuked me and who spit on me. (Is 50:6)
Hail Mary…

Behold, my servant will understand; he will be exalted and lifted up, and he will be very sublime. (Is 52:13)
Hail Mary…

Many were astonished when they saw him, his appearance was so disfigured more than any man, and his form was beyond human. (Is 52:14)
Hail Mary…

He shall startle many nations, kings shall shut their mouth because of him: that which had not been told them, they will see; and that which they had not known, they will understand. (Is 52:15)
Hail Mary…

He was lifted up from anguish and judgment. Who will describe his life? For he has been cut off from the land of the living. Because of the wickedness of my people, I have struck him down. (Is 53:8)
Hail Mary…

He will be given a place with the impious for his burial, and with the rich for his death, though he has done no iniquity, nor was deceit in his mouth. (Is 53:9)
Hail Mary…

It was the will of the Lord to crush him with infirmity. If he lays down his life because of sin, he will see offspring with long lives, and the will of the Lord will be directed by his hand. (Is 53:10)
Hail Mary…

His reign will be increased, and there will be no end to his peace. He will sit upon the throne of David and over his kingdom, to confirm and strengthen

it, in judgment and justice, from now even unto eternity. The zeal of the Lord of hosts shall accomplish this. (Is 9:7)
Hail Mary...

I shall see him, but not presently. I shall gaze upon him, but not soon. A star shall rise out of Jacob, and a rod shall spring up from Israel. (Num 24:17)
Hail Mary...

Glory Be...

Prophecies about Jesus II

Decade 1
Our Father…

John was clothed with camel's hair, with a leather belt around his waist, and he ate locusts and wild honey. He proclaimed, "The one who is more powerful than I is coming after me; I am not worthy to stoop down and untie the thong of his sandals. I have baptized you with water; but he will baptize you with the Holy Spirit." (Mrk 1:6-8)
Hail Mary…

The eyes of the blind will be opened, and the ears of the deaf will be cleared. Then the disabled will leap like a dear, and the tongue of the mute will be untied. For the waters have burst forth in the wilderness, and streams in the desert. (Is 35:5-6)
Hail Mary…

The Spirit of the Lord is upon me, for the Lord has anointed me. He has sent me to bring good news to the meek, so as to heal the contrite of heart, to proclaim liberty to captives and release to the confined, and so to proclaim the acceptable year of the Lord and the day of vindication of our God: to console all who are mourning. (Is 61:1-2)
Hail Mary…

Moses called all the elders of Israel, and he said to them: "Go, taking an animal by your families, and sacrifice the Passover. And dip a little bundle of hyssop in the blood which is at the entrance, and sprinkle the upper threshold with it, and both of the door posts. Let none of you go out of the door of his house until morning. For the Lord will cross through, striking the Egyptians. And when he will see the blood on the upper threshold, and on both the door posts, he will pass over the door of the house and not permit the Striker to enter into your houses or to do harm. (Exo 12:21-23)
Hail Mary…

My friends and my companions stand aloof from my plague. And they that were near me stood afar off: They that sought my life lay snares for me, and those who sought to hurt me spoke vain things and meditate deceits all day long. (Ps 38:11-12/Ps 37:12-13)
Hail Mary…

All who hate me whispered together against me: they devised evil against me. An evil thing, say they, has cleaved fast unto me, and I shall lie and not rise again. For even a familiar friend, in whom I trusted, who ate of my bread, has lifted his heel against me. (Ps 41:7-9 / Ps 40:8-10)
Hail Mary...

He will cast down violently, on this mountain, the face of the chains, with which all peoples had been bound, and the net, with which all nations had been covered. He will violently cast down death forever. And the Lord God will take away the tears from every face, and he will take away the disgrace of his people from the entire earth. (Is 25:7-8)
Hail Mary...

I will raise me up a faithful priest, who shall do according to what is in my heart, and in my mind, and I will build him a sure house, and he shall walk before my anointed one forever. (1 Sam 2:35)
Hail Mary...

Some from that crowd, when they had heard these words of his, were saying, "This one truly is the Prophet." Others were saying, "He is the Christ." Yet certain ones were saying: "Does the Christ come from Galilee? Does Scripture not say that the Christ comes from the offspring of David and from Bethlehem, the town where David was?" (Jn 7:40-42)
Hail Mary...

The stone which the builders have rejected, this has become the chief cornerstone. By the Lord has this been done, and it is a wonder before our eyes. (Ps 118:22-23)
Hail Mary...

Glory Be…

Decade 2
Our Father…

Go through, go through the gates! Prepare a way for the people! Make the road level, remove the stones, and lift up a sign for the people! Behold, the Lord has caused it to be heard to the ends of the earth. Tell the daughter of Zion: "Behold, your Savior approaches! Behold, his reward is with him, and his work before him." (Is 62:10-11)
Hail Mary...

The Spirit of the Lord will rest upon him: the spirit of wisdom and understanding, the spirit of counsel and fortitude, the spirit of knowledge and piety. And he will be filled with the spirit of the fear of the Lord. He will

not judge according to the sight of the eyes, nor reprove according to the hearing of the ears. (Is 11:2-3)
Hail Mary...

The Lord said to my Lord, "Sit at my right hand, until I make your enemies your footstool." (Ps 110:1)
Hail Mary...

The Lord has sworn, and will not change his mind: "You are a priest forever, according to the order of Melchizedek." (Ps 110:4)
Hail Mary...

The Lord is at your right hand. He has shattered kings in the day of his wrath. He will judge between the nations; he will heap up corpses. He will shatter heads in the land of the many. He will drink from the stream on the way. Because of this, he will lift up his head. (Ps 110:5-7)
Hail Mary...

I say to you, that what has been written must still be fulfilled in me: 'And he was esteemed with the wicked.' and indeed what is written about me is being fulfilled. (Luk 22:37)
Hail Mary...

I will grant wonders in the sky and on earth: blood and fire and the vapor of smoke. The sun will be turned into darkness, and the moon into blood, before the great and terrible day of the Lord shall arrive. (Joel 2:30-31)
Hail Mary...

It will happen that everyone who will call upon the name of the Lord will be saved. For on Mount Zion, and in Jerusalem, and in the remnant whom the Lord will call, there will be salvation, just as the Lord has said. (Joel 2:32)
Hail Mary...

Awake, O spear, against my shepherd and against the man that clings to me, says the Lord of hosts. Strike the shepherd, and the sheep will be scattered. (Zech 13:7)
Hail Mary...

He will judge the poor of the people, and he will bring salvation to the needy. And he will humble the false accuser. And he will remain, with the sun and before the moon, from generation to generation. (Ps 72:4-5)
Hail Mary...

Glory Be...

Decade 3

Our Father…

He will descend like rain upon fleece, and like showers showering upon the earth. In his days, justice will rise like the sun, with abundance of peace, until the moon is taken away. And he will rule from sea to sea and from the river to the limits of the whole world. (Ps 72:6-8)
Hail Mary…

In his sight, the Ethiopians will fall prostrate, and his enemies will lick the ground. The kings of Tarshish and the islands will offer gifts. The kings of Arabia and of Seba will bring gifts. And all the kings of the earth shall adore him. All nations will serve him. (Ps 72:9-11)
Hail Mary…

He will free the poor from the powerful, and the poor one who has no helper. He will spare the poor and the indigent, and he will bring salvation to the souls of the poor. He will redeem their souls from oppression and from iniquity, and their names shall be honorable in his sight. (Ps 72:12-14)
Hail Mary…

Permit me to speak freely to you about our ancestor David: for he passed away and was buried, and his tomb is with us, even to this very day. Therefore, he was a prophet, for he knew that God had sworn an oath to him that he would put one of his descendants on his throne. Foreseeing this, he was speaking about the Resurrection of the Christ. 'He was not abandoned to Hades, nor did his flesh experience corruption.' This Jesus, God raised up again, and of this we are all witnesses. (Acts 2:29-32)
Hail Mary…

Behold, the days are approaching, says the Lord, when I will form a new covenant with the house of Israel and with the house of Judah, not according to the covenant which I made with their fathers, in the day when I took them by the hand, so as to lead them away from the land of Egypt, the covenant which they nullified, though I was the ruler over them, says the Lord. (Jer 31:31-32)
Hail Mary…

Why have the nations raged, and the people devised vain plots? The kings of the earth stood up, and the princes met together, against the Lord and against his anointed, saying, "Let us break their bonds asunder: and let us cast away their yoke from us." (Ps 2:1-3)
Hail Mary…

He who sits in the heavens shall laugh: the Lord shall have them in derision. Then shall he speak to them in his wrath, and terrify them in his fury, saying, "I have set my king upon my holy hill of Zion." (Ps 2:4-6)
Hail Mary…

The Lord has said to me: You are my son, this day have I begotten you. (Ps 2:7)
Hail Mary…

Ask of me and I will give to you: the Gentiles for your inheritance, and the ends of the earth for your possession. You will rule them with an iron rod, and you will shatter them like a potter's vessel. (Ps 2:8-9)
Hail Mary…

Lord, you are the One who made heaven and earth, the sea and all that is in them, who, by the Holy Spirit, through the mouth of our father David, your servant, said: 'Why have the Gentiles been raging, and why have the people been pondering vain things? The kings of the earth have stood up, and the leaders have joined together as one, against the Lord and against his messiah.' (Acts 4:24-26)
Hail Mary…

Glory Be…

Decade 4
Our Father…

When they had appointed a day for him, great numbers went to him at his lodging. And he explained, testifying to the kingdom of God, and persuading them about Jesus, using the law of Moses and the Prophets. (Acts 28:23)
Hail Mary…

When he had arrived, he held many discussions with those who had believed. For he was vehemently and publicly reproving the Jews, by revealing through the Scriptures that Jesus is the Christ. (Acts 18:27-28)
Hail Mary…

Your throne, O God, is forever and ever. The scepter of your kingdom is a scepter for justice. You have loved justice and hated iniquity. Because of this, God, your God, has anointed you, before your co-heirs, with the oil of gladness. (Ps 45:6-7)
Hail Mary…

I will be a father to him, and he shall be a son to me. And I will not take away my mercy from him, as I took it away from the one who was before you. And I will station him in my house and in my kingdom forever. And his throne will be established forever. (1 Chron 17:13)
Hail Mary…

I have endured reproach; confusion has covered my face. I have become a stranger to my kindred and an alien to my mother's children. For zeal for your house has consumed me, and the reproaches of those who reproached you have fallen upon me. (Ps 69:8-10)
Hail Mary…

O Lord, our Lord, how admirable is your name throughout all the earth! For your magnificence is elevated above the heavens. Out of the mouths of babes and infants, you have perfected praise, because of your enemies, so that you may destroy the enemy and the avenger. (Ps 8:2-3)
Hail Mary…

Go forth! And you shall say to this people: 'When you listen, you will hear and not understand. And when you see a vision, you will not comprehend.' Blind the heart of this people. Make their ears heavy and close their eyes, lest they see with their eyes, and hear with their ears, and understand with their heart, and be converted, and then I would heal them. (Is 6:9-10)
Hail Mary…

They will rejoice before you, like those who rejoice at the harvest, like the victorious exulting after capturing the prey, when they divide the spoils. For you have prevailed over the yoke of their burden, and over the rod of their shoulder, and over the scepter of their oppressor. (Is 9:3-4)
Hail Mary…

Thus says the Lord: "A voice has been heard on high: of lamentation, mourning, and weeping; of Rachel crying for her children and refusing to be consoled over them, because they are no more." (Jer 31:15)
Hail Mary…

I saw their ways, and I will heal them, and I will lead them back again, and I will restore consolations to them and to those who mourn for them, I will create the fruit of the lips: peace, peace to them who are far away, and peace to them who are near, says the Lord, and I will heal them. (Is 57:18-19)
Hail Mary...

Glory Be…

Decade 5
Our Father…

Behold, I will lead over them scars and health, and I will cure them. And I will reveal to them an invocation of peace and truth. (Jer 33:6)
Hail Mary…

Thus says the Lord God: Behold, I myself will seek my sheep, and I myself will visit them. (Eze 34:11)
Hail Mary…

Just as a shepherd visits his flock, in the day when he will be in the midst of his sheep that were scattered, so will I visit my sheep. And I will deliver them from all the places to which they had been scattered in the day of gloom and darkness. (Eze 34:12)
Hail Mary…

I myself will be the shepherd of my sheep, and I will make them lie down, says the Lord God. (Eze 34:15)
Hail Mary…

I will seek what had been lost. And I will lead back again what had been cast aside. And I will bind up what had been broken. And I will strengthen what had been infirm. (Eze 34:16)
Hail Mary…

There was a prophet, Anna, a daughter of Phanuel, from the tribe of Asher. She was very advanced in years, and she had lived with her husband for seven years after her marriage then as a widow to the age of eighty-four. And without departing from the temple, she worshipped there with fasting and prayer, night and day. At that moment she came and she praised the Lord. And she spoke about the child to all who were awaiting the redemption of Israel. (Luk 2:36-38)
Hail Mary…

John saw Jesus coming toward him, and so he said: "Behold, the Lamb of God. Behold, he who takes away the sin of the world. This is the one about whom I said, 'After me comes a man, who has been placed ahead of me, because he existed before me.' And I did not know him. Yet it is for this reason that I come baptizing with water: so that he may be revealed in Israel." (Jn 1:29-31)
Hail Mary…

I keep the Lord always in my sight. For he is at my right hand, so that I may not be moved. Because of this, my heart has been joyful, and my tongue has

exulted. Moreover, even my body will rest in hope. For you will not abandon my soul to Hell, nor will you allow your holy one to see corruption. (Ps 16:8-10)
Hail Mary…

This shall be a sign and a testimony to the Lord of hosts in the land of Egypt. For they will cry out to the Lord because of oppressors, and he will send them a savior and a defender who will free them. (Is 19:20)
Hail Mary…

I was like a meek lamb led to the slaughter. And I did not realize that they had devised plans against me, saying: "Let us destroy the tree with its fruit, and let us eradicate him from the land of the living, and let his name no longer be remembered." (Jer 11:19)
Hail Mary…

Glory Be…

Who is Jesus? (part 1)

Decade 1
Our Father…

In the past, God spoke to our ancestors in many and various ways through the prophets, but in these last days he has spoken to us by his Son, whom he has appointed heir of all things, by whom also he created the universe. (Heb 1:1-2)
Hail Mary…

He reflects the brightness of God's glory and the likeness of his very being, and he sustains all things by his powerful word. After making purification for our sins, he sat down at the right hand of the majesty on high. (Heb 1:3)
Hail Mary…

This man, offering one sacrifice for sins, sits at the right hand of God forever, awaiting that time when his enemies will be made his footstool. (Heb 10:12-13)
Hail Mary…

You know the grace of our Lord Jesus Christ, that though he was rich, he became poor for your sakes, so that through his poverty, you might become rich. (2 Cor 8:9)
Hail Mary…

Though he was in the form of God, did not consider equality with God something to be exploited. Instead, he emptied himself, taking the form of a servant, being made in the likeness of men, and accepting the state of a man. He humbled himself, becoming obedient even unto death, even the death of the Cross. (Phil 2:6-8)
Hail Mary…

God has also exalted him and has given him a name which is above every name, so that, at the name of Jesus, every knee would bend, of those in heaven, of those on earth, and of those in hell, and so that every tongue would confess that the Lord Jesus Christ is in the glory of God the Father. (Phil 2:9-11)
Hail Mary…

Christ who was offered once to bear the sins of many, shall appear a second time, not to take away sin, but to bring salvation to those who are eagerly waiting for him. (Heb 9:28)
Hail Mary...

When the fullness of time arrived, God sent his Son, formed from a woman, formed under the law, so that he might redeem those who were under the law, in order that we might receive adoption as children. (Gal 4:4-5)
Hail Mary...

He is the image of the invisible God, the first-born of every creature. For in him was created everything in heaven and on earth, visible and invisible, whether thrones, or dominions, or principalities, or powers. All things were created through him and in him. (Col 1:15-16)
Hail Mary...

Christ existed before all things, and in union with him all things have their proper place. He is the head of his body, the church; he is the source of the body's life. He is the first-born Son, who was raised from death, in order that he alone might have the first place in all things. (Col 1:17-18)
Hail Mary...

Glory Be...

Decade 2
Our Father...

The Father is well-pleased that all fullness reside in him, and that, through him, all things be reconciled to himself, making peace through the blood of his cross, for the things that are on earth, as well as the things that are in heaven. (Col 1:19-20)
Hail Mary...

Christ has redeemed us from the curse of the law, since he became a curse for us. For it is written: "Cursed is anyone who hangs from a tree." (Gal 3:13)
Hail Mary...

Christ was without sin, but for our sake God made him share our sin so that we might become the righteousness of God. (2 Cor 5:21)
Hail Mary...

Be it known therefore to you, that through him forgiveness of sins is preached to you. By this Jesus, everyone who believes is set free from those sins, from which you could not be set free by the law of Moses. (Acts 13:38-39)

Hail Mary…

You know that it was not with corruptible gold or silver that you were redeemed away from your useless behavior in the traditions of your fathers, but it was with the precious blood of Christ, an immaculate and undefiled lamb. (1 Pet 1:18-19)
Hail Mary…

He had been chosen by God before the foundation of the world, but manifested in the last times for you. Through him you believe in God, who raised him up from the dead, and has given him glory, so that your faith and hope are set on God. (1 Pet 1:20-21)
Hail Mary…

We understand that Jesus, who was reduced to a little less than the Angels, was crowned with glory and honor because of his Passion and death, in order that, by the grace of God, he might taste death for all. (Heb 2:9)
Hail Mary…

Since therefore the children are partakers of flesh and blood, Jesus also himself in like manner has been partaker of the same, so that, through death, he might destroy the devil who has the power over death. And deliver those who all their lives were held in slavery by the fear of death. (Heb 2:14-15)
Hail Mary…

It is fitting for him to become like his people in all things, so that he might become a merciful and faithful High Priest before God, in order that he might bring forgiveness to the sins of the people. (Heb 2:17)
Hail Mary…

We do not have a high priest who is unable to have compassion on our infirmities, but rather one who was tempted in all things, just as we are, yet without sin. (Heb 4:15)
Hail Mary…

Glory Be…

Decade 3
Our Father…

It is Christ who, in the days of his flesh, with a strong cry and tears, offered prayers and supplications to the One who was able to save him from death, and who was heard because of his reverence. (Heb 5:7)
Hail Mary…

Although, he is the Son of God, he learned obedience by the things that he suffered. And having reached perfection, he was made the source of eternal salvation for all who are obedient to him, having been called by God to be the High Priest, according to the order of Melchizedek. (Heb 5:8-10)
Hail Mary…

Come to the Lord, a living stone rejected by people, but chosen and honored by God. (1 Pet 2:4)
Hail Mary…

Christ also died once for our sins, the Just One on behalf of the unjust, so that he might offer us to God, having died in the flesh, but having been made alive in the Spirit. (1 Pet 3:18)
Hail Mary…

Jesus did not enter by means of holy things made with hands, mere examples of the true things, but he entered into Heaven itself, so that he may appear now before the face of God for us. (Heb 9:24)
Hail Mary…

When as yet we were weak, at the right time, Christ died for the ungodly. For rarely for a just man will anyone die; though perhaps for a good man someone would actually dare to die. (Rom 5:6-7)
Hail Mary…

While we were still enemies of God, if we were reconciled to Him through the death of his Son, all the more so, having been reconciled, shall we be saved by Christ's life. (Rom 5:10)
Hail Mary…

We know that Christ, in rising up from the dead, can no longer die: death no longer has dominion over him. For in as much as he died for sin, he died once. But in as much as he lives, he lives for God. (Rom 6:9-10)
Hail Mary…

There is one God, and one mediator of God and of men, the man Christ Jesus, who gave himself as a redemption for all, as a testimony in its proper time. (1 Tim 2:5-6)
Hail Mary…

Jesus is the one of whom the scripture says, 'The stone that you the builders rejected turned out to be the cornerstone.' There is no salvation in any other. For there is no other name under heaven given to men, by which we must be saved. (Acts 4:11-12)
Hail Mary…

Glory Be…

Decade 4
Our Father…

These shall fight against the Lamb, and the Lamb shall conquer them. For he is the Lord of lords and the King of kings. And those who are with him are called, and chosen, and faithful. (Rev 17:14)
Hail Mary…

For if you confess with your mouth the Lord Jesus, and if you believe in your heart that God has raised him up from the dead, you shall be saved. (Rom 10:9)
Hail Mary…

I am the Alpha and the Omega, the First and the Last, the Beginning and the End. (Rev 22:13)
Hail Mary…

Let us run with perseverance the race that is set before us, looking unto Jesus the author and finisher of our faith, who for the joy that was set before him endured the cross, despising the shame, and has taken his seat at the right hand of the throne of God. (Heb 12:1-2)
Hail Mary…

He is the atoning sacrifice for our sins. And not only for our sins, but also for those of the whole world. (1 Jn 2:2)
Hail Mary…

This man, because he continues forever, has an everlasting priesthood. And for this reason, he is able, continuously, to save those who approach God through him, since he is ever alive to make intercession on our behalf. (Heb 7:24-25)
Hail Mary…

God did not send his Son into the world, in order to judge the world, but in order that the world may be saved through him. (Jn 3:17)
Hail Mary…

Jesus Christ is the same yesterday, today, and forever. (Heb 13:8)
Hail Mary…

We know that the Son of God has arrived, and that he has given us understanding, so that we may know the true God, and so that we may remain in his true Son. This is the true God, and this is Eternal Life. (1 Jn 5:20)

Hail Mary…

He has been granted a better ministry, so much so that he is also the Mediator of a better testament, which has been confirmed by better promises. (Heb 8:6)
Hail Mary…

Glory Be…

Decade 5
Our Father…

He was with God in the beginning. (Jn 1:2)
Hail Mary…

All things were made through Him, and nothing that was made was made without Him. (Jn 1:3)
Hail Mary…

In him was life, and the life was the light of all people. (Jn 1:3-4)
Hail Mary…

He was in the world, and the world was made through him, and the world did not recognize him. (Jn 1:10)
Hail Mary…

He went to his own, and his own did not accept him. (Jn 1:11)
Hail Mary…

Yet whoever did accept him, those who believed in his name, he gave them the power to become children of God. These are born, not of blood, nor of the will of flesh, nor of the will of man, but of God. (Jn 1:12-13)
Hail Mary…

And the Word became flesh, and he lived among us, and we saw his glory, glory like that of an only-begotten Son from the Father, full of grace and truth. (Jn 1:14)
Hail Mary…

John spoke about him and cried out, "This is he of whom I spoke, 'He who shall come after me, is greater than I am, because he was before me.'" From his fulness we have all received, grace after grace. (Jn 1:15-16)
Hail Mary…

The law was given through Moses, but grace and truth came through Jesus Christ. (Jn 1:17)

Hail Mary…

No man has ever seen God. The only begotten Son, who is God, and who is at the Father's side, he has made him known. (Jn 1:18)
Hail Mary…

Glory Be…

Who is Jesus? (part II)

Decade 1
Our Father…

If we walk in the light, just as he also is in the light, then we have fellowship with one another, and the blood of Jesus Christ, his Son, cleanses us from all sin. (1 Jn 1:7)
Hail Mary…

My little children, this I write to you, so that you may not sin. But if anyone has sinned, we have an Advocate with the Father, Jesus Christ, the Just One. (1 Jn 2:1)
Hail Mary…

This is his commandment: that we should believe in the name of his Son, Jesus Christ, and love one another, just as he has commanded us. (1 Jn 3:23)
Hail Mary…

The Spirit of God may be known in this way. Every spirit who confesses that Jesus Christ has arrived in the flesh is of God; and every spirit who contradicts Jesus is not of God. (1 Jn 4:2-3)
Hail Mary…

We have seen, and we testify, that the Father has sent his Son to be the Savior of the world. Whoever has confessed that Jesus is the Son of God, God abides in him, and he in God. (1 Jn 4:14-15)
Hail Mary…

Whosoever believes that Jesus is the Christ, is born of God. And everyone who loves the parent, also loves whoever has been born of him. (1 Jn 5:1)
Hail Mary…

This is he who came by water and blood, Jesus Christ: not by water only, but by water and blood. And the Spirit is the one who testifies, because the Spirit is the truth (1 Jn 5:6)
Hail Mary…

I pray that Christ may dwell by faith in your hearts; that being rooted and founded in love, you may be able to comprehend, with all God's people, what is the breadth, and length, and height, and depth of Christ's love, that surpasses all knowledge. (Eph 3:17-19)
Hail Mary…

You also are saved, in a similar manner, by baptism, not by the testimony of sordid flesh, but by the examination of a good conscience in God, through the resurrection of Jesus Christ. He is at the right hand of God, devouring death, so that we may be made heirs to eternal life. (1 Pet 3:21-22)
Hail Mary…

Blessed be the God and Father of our Lord Jesus Christ, who according to his great mercy has regenerated us into a living hope, through the resurrection of Jesus Christ from the dead: unto an incorruptible and undefiled and unfading inheritance, which is reserved for you in heaven. (1 Pet 1:3-4)
Hail Mary…

Glory Be…

Decade 2
Our Father…

He who sanctifies, and those who are sanctified, are all from One. For this reason, he is not ashamed to call them brothers, saying: "I will announce your name to my brothers. In the midst of the Church, I will praise you." (Heb 2:11-12)
Hail Mary…

Holy brothers and sisters, sharers in the heavenly calling, consider the Apostle and High Priest of our confession: Jesus. He is faithful to the One who made him, just as Moses also was, with his entire house. For this Jesus was considered worthy of greater glory than Moses, so much so that the house which he has built holds a greater honor than the former one. (Heb 3:1-2)
Hail Mary…

Since we have a great High Priest, who has pierced the heavens, Jesus the Son of God, we should hold fast to our confession. (Heb 4:14)
Hail Mary…

This we have as an anchor of the soul, safe and sound, which advances even to the interior of the veil, to the place where the forerunner Jesus has entered on our behalf, so as to become the High Priest for eternity, according to the order of Melchizedek. (Heb 6:20)
Hail Mary…

Do not be ashamed of the testimony of our Lord, nor of me, his prisoner. Instead, join with me in suffering for the Gospel with the strength that comes from God, who has freed us and has called us to his holy vocation, not

according to our works, but according to his own purpose and grace, which was given to us in Christ Jesus, before the ages began. (2 tim 1:8-9)
Hail Mary...

"I, Jesus, have sent my Angel, to testify to these things for you among the Churches. I am the Root and the Origin of David, the bright morning Star." (Rev 22:16)
Hail Mary...

Jesus, too, in order to sanctify the people by his own blood, suffered outside the gate. And so, let us go forth to him, outside the camp, bearing his reproach. For in this place, we have no everlasting city; instead, we seek one in the future. (Heb 13:12-14)
Hail Mary...

If the blood of goats and oxen, and the ashes of a calf, when these are sprinkled, sanctify those who have been defiled, in order to cleanse the flesh, how much more will the blood of Christ, who through the Holy Spirit has offered himself, immaculate, to God, cleanse our conscience from dead works, in order to serve the living God? (Heb 9:13-15)
Hail Mary...

God, having looked down to see the ignorance of these times, has now announced to men that everyone everywhere should do penance. For he has appointed a day on which he will judge the world in equity, through the man whom he has appointed, offering faith to all, by raising him from the dead. (Acts 17:30-31)
Hail Mary...

Having therefore, a confidence to enter into the sanctuary by the blood of Christ, a new and living way which he opened for us through the veil, that is to say, his flesh, and since we have a high priest over the house of God, let us draw near with a true heart in fulness of faith, having our hearts sprinkled from an evil conscience, and our bodies washed with pure water. (Heb 10:19-22)
Hail Mary...

Glory Be...

Decade 3
Our Father...

God poured forth his Holy Spirit upon us abundantly, through Jesus Christ our Savior, so that, by being justified by his grace, we may become heirs, according to the hope of eternal life. (Tit 3:6-7)
Hail Mary…

He received honor and glory from God the Father, whose voice descended to him from the magnificent glory: "This is my beloved Son, in whom I am well pleased. Listen to him." We also heard this voice conveyed from heaven, when we were with him on the holy mountain. (2 Pet 1:17-18)
Hail Mary…

Everyone who withdraws and does not remain in the teaching of Christ, does not have God. Whoever remains in the teaching, such a one as this has both the Father and the Son. (2 Jn 1:9)
Hail Mary…

Blessed is the Lord God of Israel. For he has visited and has brought the redemption of his people. And he has raised up a horn of salvation for us, in the house of David his servant. (Luk 1:68-69)
Hail Mary…

In the beginning was the Word, and the Word was with God, and the Word was God. (Jn 1:1)
Hail Mary…

In this is love: it is not as though we have loved God, but because he first loved us, and sent his Son to be a propitiation for our sins. (1 Jn 4:10)
Hail Mary…

In Him was life, and Life was the light of men. And the light shines in the darkness, and the darkness did not overcome it. (Jn 1:4-5)
Hail Mary…

I baptize with water. But in your midst stands one, whom you do not know. The one who is to come after me, who has been placed ahead of me, the straps of whose sandle I am not worthy to untie. (Jn 1:26-27)
Hail Mary…

The woman said to him: "I know that the Messiah is coming (who is called the Christ). And then, when he will have arrived, he will announce everything to us." Jesus said to her: "I am he, the one who is speaking with you." (Jn 4:25-26)
Hail Mary…

God has not destined us for wrath, but for obtaining salvation through our Lord Jesus Christ, who died for us, so that, whether we are awake, or whether we sleep, we may live in union with him. (1 Thes 5:9-10)
Hail Mary...

Glory Be...

Decade 4
Our Father...

You yourselves thoroughly understand that the day of the Lord shall arrive much like a thief in the night. For when they will say, "Peace and security!" then destruction will suddenly overwhelm them, like the labor pains of a woman with child, and they will not escape. (1 Thes 5:2-3)
Hail Mary...

I saw heaven opened, and behold, a white horse. And he who was sitting upon it was called Faithful and True. And with justice does he judge and fight. And his eyes are like a flame of fire, and on his head are many diadems, having a name written, which no one knows except himself. And he was clothed with a vestment sprinkled with blood. And his name is called: THE WORD OF GOD. (Rev 19:11-13)
Hail Mary...

From his mouth proceeded a sharp two-edged sword, so that with it he may strike the nations. And he shall rule them with an iron rod. And he treads the winepress of the fury of the wrath of God Almighty. And he has on his garment and on his thigh written: KING OF KINGS AND LORD OF LORDS. (Rev 19:15-16)
Hail Mary...

He has rescued us from the power of darkness, and he has transferred us into the kingdom of the Son of his love, in whom we have redemption through his blood, the remission of sins. (Col 1:13-14)
Hail Mary...

Through Christ, he has given us the greatest and most precious promises, so that by these things you may become sharers in the Divine Nature, fleeing from the corruption of that desire which is in the world. (2 Pet 1:4)
Hail Mary...

God proves his love for us in that, while we were yet sinners, at the proper time, Christ died for us. Therefore, having been justified now by his blood, all the more so shall we be saved from wrath through him. (Rom 5:8-9)
Hail Mary...

For though by the offense of one, many died, yet much more so, by the grace of one man, Jesus Christ, has the grace and gift of God abounded to many. (Rom 5:15)
Hail Mary...

For though, by the one offense, death reigned through one, yet so much more so shall those who receive an abundance of grace and the free gift of righteousness exercise dominion in life through the one man, Jesus Christ. (Rom 5:17)
Hail Mary...

Whoever conquers, I will grant to him to sit with me on my throne, just as I also have conquered and have sat down with my Father on his throne. (Rev 3:21)
Hail Mary...

When I had seen him, I fell at his feet, like one who is dead. And he laid his right hand upon me, saying: Do not be afraid. I am the First and the Last. And I am alive, though I was dead. And, behold, I live forever and ever. And I hold the keys of death and of Hell. (Rev 1:17-18)
Hail Mary...

Glory Be...

Decade 5
Our Father...

Behold, he arrives with the clouds, and every eye shall see him, even those who pierced him. And all the tribes of the earth shall lament for themselves over him. So it is to be. Amen. "I am the Alpha and the Omega, the Beginning and the End," says the Lord God, who is, and who was, and who is to come, the Almighty. (Rev 1:7-8)
Hail Mary...

Jesus Christ, who is the faithful witness, the first-born of the dead, and the leader over the kings of the earth, who has loved us and has washed us from our sins with his blood, and who has made us into a kingdom and into priests for God and for his Father. To him be glory and dominion forever and ever. (Rev 1:5-6)
Hail Mary...

It was not by following cleverly devised myths that we made known to you the power and presence of our Lord Jesus Christ, but we were made eyewitnesses of his greatness. (2 Pet 1:16)
Hail Mary...

Whoever commits sin is of the devil. For the devil sins from the beginning. For this reason, the Son of God appeared, so that he might destroy the works of the devil. (1 Jn 3:8)
Hail Mary…

Whoever believes in the Son of God, holds the testimony of God within himself. Whoever does not believe in the Son, makes him a liar, because he does not believe in the testimony which God has testified about his Son. And this is the testimony which God has given to us: Eternal Life. And this Life is in his Son. (1 Jn 5:10-11)
Hail Mary…

Whoever has the Son, has Life. Whoever does not have the Son, does not have Life. (1 Jn 5:12)
Hail Mary…

The saying is trustworthy, and worthy of acceptance by everyone, that Christ Jesus came into this world to bring salvation to sinners, among whom I am the foremost. (1 Tim 1:15)
Hail Mary…

He was manifested in the flesh, was justified in the spirit, seen by angels, proclaimed among the Gentiles, believed in the world, taken up in glory. (1 Tim 3:16)
Hail Mary…

The love of God was made apparent to us in this way: that God sent his only-begotten Son into the world, so that we might live through him. (1 Jn 4:9)
Hail Mary…

Be imitators of God. And walk in love, just as Christ also loved us and gave himself for us, as a fragrant offering and sacrifice to God. (Eph 5:1-2)
Hail Mary…

Glory Be…

Passion Rosary I

According to the Gospel of Matthew (Synoptic Gospels)

Decade 1
Our Father…

While he was still speaking, behold, Judas, one of the twelve, arrived, and with him was a large crowd with swords and clubs, sent from the leaders of the priests and the elders of the people. (Matt 26:47)
Hail Mary…

He who betrayed him gave them a sign, saying: "Whomever I will kiss, it is he. Take hold of him." And quickly drawing close to Jesus, he said, "Hail, Master." And he kissed him. (Matt 26:48-49)
Hail Mary…

Jesus said to him, "Friend, for what purpose have you come?" Then they approached, and they put their hands on Jesus, and they arrested him. (Matt 26:50)
Hail Mary…

Behold, one of those who were with Jesus, extending his hand, drew his sword and struck the servant of the high priest, cutting off his ear. (Matt 26:51)
Hail Mary…

Then Jesus said to him: "Put your sword back in its place. For all who take up the sword shall perish by the sword." (Matt 26:52)
Hail Mary…

Do you think that I cannot ask my Father, so that he would give me, even now, more than twelve legions of Angels? How then would the Scriptures be fulfilled, which say that it must be so? (Matt 26:53-54)
Hail Mary…

In that same hour, Jesus said to the crowds: "You went out, as if to a robber, with swords and clubs to seize me. Yet I sat daily with you, teaching in the temple, and you did not take hold of me. (Matt 26:55)
Hail Mary…

But all this has happened so that the Scriptures of the prophets may be fulfilled. Then all the disciples fled, abandoning him. (Matt 26:56)
Hail Mary...

Those who were holding Jesus led him to Caiaphas, the high priest, where the scribes and the elders had joined together. (Matt 26:57)
Hail Mary...

Then Peter followed him from a distance, as far as the court of the high priest. And going inside, he sat down with the servants, so that he might see the end. (Matt 26:58)
Hail Mary...

Glory Be...

Decade 2
Our Father...

Then the leaders of the priests and the entire council sought false testimony against Jesus, so that they might deliver him to death. (Matt 26:59)
Hail Mary...

And they did not find any, even though many false witnesses had come forward. Then, at the very end, two false witnesses came forward, and they said, "This man said: 'I am able to destroy the temple of God, and, after three days, to rebuild it.' " (Matt 26:60-61)
Hail Mary...

And the high priest, rising up, said to him, "Have you nothing to respond to what these ones testify against you?" (Matt 26:62)
Hail Mary...

But Jesus was silent. And the high priest said to him, "I bind you by an oath to the living God to tell us if you are the Christ, the Son of God." (Matt 26:63)
Hail Mary...

Jesus said to him: "You have said it. Yet truly I say to you, hereafter you shall see the Son of man sitting at the right hand of the power of God, and coming on the clouds of heaven." (Matt 26:64)
Hail Mary...

Then the high priest tore his garments, saying: "He has blasphemed. Why do we still need witnesses? Behold, you have now heard the blasphemy. So they responded by saying, "He is guilty unto death." (Matt 26:65-66)
Hail Mary...

Then they spit in his face, and they struck him with fists. And others struck his face with the palms of their hands, saying: "Prophesy for us, O Christ. Who is the one that struck you?" (Matt 26:67-68)
Hail Mary…

When morning arrived, all the leaders of the priests and the elders of the people took counsel against Jesus, so that they might deliver him to death. (Matt 27:1)
Hail Mary…

And they led him, bound, and handed him over to Pontius Pilate, the governor. (Matt 27:2)
Hail Mary…

Then Judas, who betrayed him, seeing that he had been condemned, regretting his conduct, brought back the thirty pieces of silver to the leaders of the priests and the elders, saying, "I have sinned in betraying just blood." But they said to him: "What is that to us? See to it yourself." (Matt 27:3-4)
Hail Mary…

Glory Be…

Decade 3
Our Father…

Throwing down the pieces of silver in the temple, he departed. And going out, he hanged himself with a snare. But the leaders of the priests, having taken up the pieces of silver, said, "It is not lawful to put them into the temple offerings, because it is the price of blood." (Matt 27:5-6)
Hail Mary…

Now Jesus stood before the governor, and the governor questioned him, saying, "You are the king of the Jews?" Jesus said to him, "You are saying so." (Matt 27:11)
Hail Mary…

When he was accused by the leaders of the priests and the elders, he responded nothing. (Matt 27:12)
Hail Mary…

Then Pilate said to him, "Do you not hear how much testimony they speak against you?" And he did not respond any word to him, so that the governor wondered greatly." (Matt 27:13-14)
Hail Mary…

Pilate said to them, "Who is it that you want me to release to you: Barabbas, or Jesus, who is called Christ?" For he knew that it was out of envy they had handed him over. (Matt 27:17-18)
Hail Mary…

As he was sitting in the place of judgment, his wife sent to him, saying: Have you nothing to do with that just man; for I have suffered many things because of a dream about him. (Matt 27:19)
Hail Mary…

The leaders of the priests and the elders persuaded the people, so that they would ask for Barabbas, and so that Jesus would be killed. Then, in response, the governor said to them, "Which of the two do you want to be released to you?" But they said to him, "Barabbas." (Matt 27:20-21)
Hail Mary…

Pilate said to them, "Then what shall I do about Jesus, who is called Christ?" They all said, "Let him be crucified." The governor said to them, "But what evil has he done?" But they cried out all the more, saying, "Let him be crucified." (Matt 27:22-23)
Hail Mary…

Then Pilate, seeing that he was able to accomplish nothing, but that a greater tumult was occurring, taking water, washed his hands in the sight of the people, saying: "I am innocent of the blood of this just man. See to it yourselves." (Matt 27:24)
Hail Mary…

The entire people responded by saying, "May his blood be upon us and upon our children." Then he released Barabbas to them. But Jesus, having been scourged, he handed over to them, so that he would be crucified. (Matt 27:25-26)
Hail Mary…

Glory Be…

Decade 4
Our Father…

Then the soldiers of the governor, taking Jesus up to the governor's headquarters, gathered the entire cohort around him. And stripping him, they put a scarlet cloak around him. (Matt 27:27-28)
Hail Mary…

Twisting some thorns into a crown, they placed it on his head, with a reed in his right hand. And genuflecting before him, they mocked him, saying, "Hail, King of the Jews." (Matt 27:29)
Hail Mary…

And spitting on him, they took the reed and struck his head. (Matt 27:30)
Hail Mary…

After they had mocked him, they stripped him of the cloak, and clothed him with his own garments, and they led him away to crucify him. (Matt 27:31)
Hail Mary…

But as they were going out, they came upon a man of Cyrene, named Simon, whom they compelled to take up his cross. (Matt 27:32)
Hail Mary…

They arrived at the place, which is called Golgotha, which is the place of Calvary. And they gave him wine to drink, mixed with gall. And when he had tasted it, he refused to drink it. (Matt 27:33-34)
Hail Mary…

Then, after they had crucified him, they divided his garments, casting lots, in order to fulfill what was spoken by the prophet, saying: "They divided my garments among them, and over my vestment they cast lots." (Matt 27:35)
Hail Mary…

But those passing by blasphemed him, shaking their heads and saying: "Ah, so you would destroy the temple of God and in three days rebuild it! Save your own self. If you are the Son of God, descend from the cross." (Matt 27:39-40)
Hail Mary…

Similarly, the leaders of the priests, with the scribes and the elders, mocking him, said: "He saved others; he cannot save himself. If he is the King of Israel, let him descend now from the cross, and we will believe in him." (Matt 27:41-42)
Hail Mary…

"He trusted in God; so now, let God free him, if he wills him. For he said, 'I am the Son of God.'" Then, the robbers who were crucified with him also reproached him with the very same thing. (Matt 27:43-44)
Hail Mary…

Glory Be…

Decade 5
Our Father...

Now from the sixth hour, there was darkness over the entire earth, even until the ninth hour. (Matt 27:45)
Hail Mary...

About the ninth hour, Jesus cried out with a loud voice, saying: "Eli, Eli, lamma sabacthani?" that is, "My God, My God, why have you forsaken me?" (Matt 27:46)
Hail Mary...

Then certain ones who were standing and listening there said, "This man calls upon Elijah. "And one of them, running quickly, took a sponge and filled it with vinegar, and he set it on a reed, and he gave it to him to drink. (Matt 27:47-48)
Hail Mary...

Yet truly, the others said, "Wait. Let us see whether Elijah will come to free him." Then Jesus, crying out again with a loud voice, gave up his life. (Matt 27:49-50)
Hail Mary...

Behold, the veil of the temple was torn into two parts, from top to bottom. And the earth was shaken, and the rocks were split apart. (Matt 27:51)
Hail Mary...

The tombs were opened. And many bodies of the saints, which had been sleeping, arose. And going out from the tombs, after his resurrection, they went into the holy city, and they appeared to many. (Matt 27:52-53)
Hail Mary...

Now the centurion and those who were with him, guarding Jesus, having seen the earthquake and the things that were done, were very fearful, saying: "Truly, this was the Son of God."(Matt 27:54)
Hail Mary...

In that place, there were many women, at a distance, who had followed Jesus from Galilee, ministering to him. Among these were Mary Magdalene and Mary the mother of James and Joseph, and the mother of the sons of Zebedee. (Matt 27:55-56)
Hail Mary...

When evening had arrived, a certain wealthy man from Arimathea, named Joseph, arrived, who himself was also a disciple of Jesus. This man

approached Pilate and asked for the body of Jesus. Then Pilate ordered the body to be released. (Matt 27:57-58)
Hail Mary…

And Joseph, taking the body, wrapped it in a clean finely woven linen cloth, and he placed it in his own new tomb, which he had hewn out of a rock. And he rolled a great stone to the door of the tomb, and he went away. (Matt 27:59-60)
Hail Mary…

Glory Be…

Passion Rosary II

According to the Gospel of John

Decade 1
Our Father...

When Jesus had said these things, he departed with his disciples across the valley of Kidron, where there was a garden, into which he entered with his disciples. But Judas, who betrayed him, also knew the place, for Jesus had frequently met with his disciples there. (Jn 18:1-2)
Hail Mary...

Then Judas, when he had received a cohort from both the high priests and the attendants of the Pharisees, approached the place with lanterns and torches and weapons. And so Jesus, knowing all that was about to happen to him, advanced and said to them, "Who are you seeking?" (Jn 18:3-4)
Hail Mary...

They answered him, "Jesus the Nazarene." Jesus said to them, "I am he." Now Judas, who betrayed him, was also standing with them. Then, when he said to them, "I am he," they moved back and fell to the ground. (Jn 18:5-6)
Hail Mary...

Then again, he questioned them: "Who are you seeking?" And they said, "Jesus the Nazarene." Jesus responded: "I told you that I am he. Therefore, if you are seeking me, permit these others to go away." (Jn 18:7-8)
Hail Mary...

Then Simon Peter, having a sword, drew it, and he struck the servant of the high priest, and he cut off his right ear. Now the name of the servant was Malchus. (Jn 18:10)
Hail Mary...

Therefore, Jesus said to Peter: "Set your sword into its sheath. Should I not drink the chalice which my Father has given to me?" (Jn 18:11)
Hail Mary...

Then the cohort, and the tribune, and the attendants of the Jews apprehended Jesus and bound him. And they led him away, first to Annas, for he was the father-in-law of Caiaphas, who was the high priest that year. (Jn 18:12-13)
Hail Mary...

Simon Peter was following Jesus with another disciple. And that disciple was known to the high priest, and so he entered with Jesus into the court of the high priest. (Jn 18:15)
Hail Mary...

The woman servant keeping the door said to Peter, "Are you not also among the disciples of this man?" He said, "I am not." (Jn 18:17)
Hail Mary...

Then the high priest questioned Jesus about his disciples and about his doctrine. Jesus responded to him: "I have spoken openly to the world. I have always taught in the synagogue and in the temple, where all the Jews meet. And I have said nothing in secret. Why do you question me? Question those who heard what I said to them. Behold, they know these things that I have said." (Jn 18:19-21)
Hail Mary...

Glory Be...

Decade 2
Our Father...

Then, when he had said this, one of the attendants standing nearby struck Jesus, saying: "Is this the way you answer the high priest?" (Jn 18:22)
Hail Mary...

Jesus answered him: "If I have spoken wrongly, offer testimony about the wrong. But if I have spoken correctly, then why do you strike me?" And Annas sent him bound to Caiaphas, the high priest. (Jn 18:23-24)
Hail Mary...

Now Simon Peter was standing and warming himself. Then they said to him, "Are you not also one of his disciples?" He denied it and said, "I am not." (Jn 18:25)
Hail Mary...

One of the servants of the high priest (a relative of him whose ear Peter had cut off) said to him, "Did I not see you in the garden with him?" Therefore, again, Peter denied it. And immediately the rooster crowed. (Jn 18:26-27)
Hail Mary...

Then they led Jesus from Caiaphas into the praetorium. Now it was morning, and so they did not enter into the praetorium, so that they would not be defiled, but might eat the Passover. (Jn 18:28)
Hail Mary…

Therefore, Pilate went outside to them, and he said, "What accusation are you bringing against this man?" They responded and said to him, "If he were not an evil-doer, we would not have handed him over to you." (Jn 18:29-30)
Hail Mary…

Pilate said to them, "Take him yourselves and judge him according to your own law." Then the Jews said to him, "It is not lawful for us to execute anyone." This was so that the word of Jesus would be fulfilled, which he spoke signifying what kind of death he would die. (Jn 18:31-32)
Hail Mary…

Then Pilate entered the headquarters again, and he called Jesus and said to him, "You are the king of the Jews?" Jesus responded, "Are you saying this of yourself, or have others spoken to you about me?" (Jn 18:33-34)
Hail Mary…

Pilate responded: "Am I a Jew? Your own nation and the high priests have handed you over to me. What have you done?" (Jn 18:35)
Hail Mary…

Jesus responded: "My kingdom is not of this world. If my kingdom were of this world, my ministers would certainly strive so that I would not be handed over to the Jews. But my kingdom is not from this world." (Jn 18:36)
Hail Mary…

Glory Be…

Decade 3
Our Father…

Pilate said to him, "You are a king, then?" Jesus answered, "You are saying that I am a king. For this I was born, and for this I came into the world: so that I may offer testimony to the truth. Everyone who is of the truth hears my voice." (Jn 18:37)
Hail Mary…

Pilate said to him, "What is truth?" And when he had said this, he went out again to the Jews, and he said to them, "I find no case against him. (Jn 18:38)
Hail Mary…

But you have a custom, that I should release someone to you at the Passover. Therefore, do you want me to release to you the king of the Jews? (Jn 18:39)
Hail Mary…

Then they all cried out repeatedly, saying: "Not this one, but Barabbas." Now Barabbas was a robber. (Jn 18:40)
Hail Mary…

Therefore, Pilate then took Jesus into custody and scourged him. (Jn 19:1)
Hail Mary…

And the soldiers, plaiting a crown of thorns, imposed it on his head. And they put a purple garment around him. And they were approaching him and saying, "Hail, king of the Jews!" And they struck him repeatedly. (Jn 19:2-3)
Hail Mary…

Then Pilate went outside again, and he said to them: "Behold, I am bringing him out to you, so that you may realize that I find no case against him." (Jn 19:4)
Hail Mary…

Then Jesus went out, bearing the crown of thorns and the purple garment. And Pilate said to them, "Behold the man." (Jn 19:5)
Hail Mary…

When the high priests and the attendants had seen him, they cried out, saying: "Crucify him! Crucify him!" Pilate said to them: "Take him yourselves and crucify him. For I find no case against him." (Jn 19:6)
Hail Mary…

The Jews answered him, "We have a law, and according to the law, he ought to die, for he has made himself the Son of God." Therefore, when Pilate had heard this word, he was more fearful. (Jn 19:7-8)
Hail Mary…

Glory Be…

Decade 4
Our Father…

He entered into the praetorium again. And he said to Jesus. "Where are you from?" But Jesus gave him no response. Therefore, Pilate said to him: "Will you not speak to me? Do you not know that I have authority to crucify you, and I have authority to release you?" (Jn 19:9-10)
Hail Mary…

Jesus responded, "You would not have any authority over me, unless it were given to you from above. For this reason, he who has handed me over to you has the greater sin." (Jn 19:11)
Hail Mary...

And from then on, Pilate was seeking to release him. But the Jews were crying out, saying: "If you release this man, you are no friend of Caesar. For anyone who makes himself a king contradicts Caesar." (Jn 19:12)
Hail Mary...

When Pilate had heard these words, he brought Jesus outside, and he sat down in the seat of judgment, in a place which is called the Pavement, but in Hebrew, it is called Gabbatha. Now it was the preparation day of the Passover, about the sixth hour. And he said to the Jews, "Behold your king." (Jn 19:13-14)
Hail Mary...

But they were crying out: "Take him away! Take him away! Crucify him!" Pilate said to them, "Shall I crucify your king?" The high priests responded, "We have no king except Caesar." (Jn 19:15)
Hail Mary...

He then handed him over to them to be crucified. And they took Jesus and led him away. And carrying his own cross, he went forth to the place, which is called Calvary, but in Hebrew it is called the Place of the Skull. (Jn 19:16-17)
Hail Mary...

There they crucified him, and with him two others, one on each side, with Jesus in the middle. (Jn 19:18)
Hail Mary...

Then Pilate also wrote a title, and he set it above the cross. And it was written: JESUS THE NAZARENE, KING OF THE JEWS. (Jn 19:19)
Hail Mary...

Then the high priests of the Jews said to Pilate: Do not write, 'King of the Jews,' but that he said, 'I am King of the Jews.' Pilate responded, "What I have written, I have written." (Jn 19:21-22)
Hail Mary...

Standing beside the cross of Jesus were his mother, and his mother's sister, and Mary of Cleophas, and Mary Magdalene. (Jn 19:25)
Hail Mary...

Glory Be…

Decade 5
Our Father…

Therefore, when Jesus had seen his mother and the disciple whom he loved standing near, he said to his mother, "Woman, behold your son." Next, he said to the disciple, "Behold your mother." And from that hour, the disciple accepted her as his own. (Jn 19:26-27)
Hail Mary…

After this, Jesus knew that all had been accomplished, so in order that the Scripture might be completed, he said, "I thirst." (Jn 19:28)
Hail Mary…

And there was a container placed there, full of vinegar. Then, placing a sponge full of vinegar around hyssop, they brought it to his mouth. Then Jesus, when he had received the vinegar, said: "It is consummated." And bowing down his head, he surrendered his spirit. (Jn 19:29-30)
Hail Mary…

Then the Jews, because it was the preparation day, so that the bodies would not remain upon the cross on the Sabbath (for that Sabbath was a great day), they petitioned Pilate in order that their legs might be broken, and they might be taken away. (Jn 19:31)
Hail Mary…

Therefore, the soldiers approached, and, indeed, they broke the legs of the first one, and of the other who was crucified with him. But after they had approached Jesus, when they saw that he was already dead, they did not break his legs. (Jn 19:32-33)
Hail Mary…

Instead, one of the soldiers opened his side with a lance, and immediately there went out blood and water. (Jn 19:34)
Hail Mary…

For these things happened so that the Scripture would be fulfilled: "You shall not break a bone of him." And again, another Scripture says: "They shall look upon him, whom they have pierced." (Jn 19:36-37)
Hail Mary…

Then, after these things, Joseph from Arimathea, (because he was a disciple of Jesus, but a secret one for fear of the Jews) petitioned Pilate so that he

might take away the body of Jesus. And Pilate gave permission. Therefore, he went and took away the body of Jesus. (Jn 19:38)
Hail Mary…

Now Nicodemus also arrived, (who had gone to Jesus at first by night) bringing a mixture of myrrh and aloe, weighing about seventy pounds. Therefore, they took the body of Jesus, and they bound it with linen cloths and the aromatic spices, just as it is the manner of the Jews to bury. (Jn 19:39-40)
Hail Mary…

Now in the place where he was crucified there was a garden, and in the garden, there was a new tomb, in which no one had yet been laid. Therefore, because of the preparation day of the Jews, since the tomb was nearby, they placed Jesus there. (Jn 19:41-42)
Hail Mary…

Glory Be…

Public Ministry of Jesus

Decade 1
Our Father...

Jesus was about thirty years old when he began his work. (Luk 3:23)
Hail Mary...

Leaving behind the city of Nazareth, he went and lived in Capernaum, near the sea, at the borders of Zebulun and of Naphtali, in order to fulfill what was said through the prophet Isaiah: "Land of Zebulun and land of Naphtali, the way of the sea across the Jordan, Galilee of the Gentiles: A people who were sitting in darkness have seen a great light. And unto those sitting in the region of the shadow of death, a light has risen." (Matt 4:13-16)
Hail Mary...

From that time, Jesus began to preach, and to say: "Repent. For the kingdom of heaven has drawn near." (Matt 4:17)
Hail Mary...

Then, seeing the crowds, he ascended the mountain, and when he had sat down, his disciples drew near to him, and opening his mouth, he taught them. (Matt 5:1-2)
Hail Mary...

Jesus traveled throughout all of Galilee, teaching in their synagogues, and preaching the Gospel of the kingdom, and healing every sickness and every infirmity among the people. (Matt 4:23)
Hail Mary...

When Jesus had completed these words, that the crowds were astonished at his doctrine. For he was teaching them as one who has authority, and not like their scribes and Pharisees. (Matt 7:28-29)
Hail Mary...

Now after John was arrested, Jesus came to Galilee, proclaiming the good news of God. (Mrk 1:14)
Hail Mary...

They entered into Capernaum. And entering into the synagogue on the Sabbath, he taught them. And they were astonished over his teaching. For he was teaching them as one who has authority, and not like the scribes. (Mrk 1:21-22)

Hail Mary...

Jesus said to them, "A prophet is not without honor, except in his own country, and in his own house, and among his own kindred." And he was not able to perform any miracles there, except that he cured a few of the infirm by laying his hands on them. And he wondered, because of their unbelief, and he traveled around in the villages, teaching. (Mrk 6:4-6)

Hail Mary...

After some days, he again entered into Capernaum. And it was heard that he was at home. So many gathered that there was no room left, not even at the door. And he spoke the word to them. (Mrk 2:1-2)

Hail Mary...

Glory Be...

Decade 2

Our Father...

Having departed, he began to preach and to spread the word, so that he was no longer able to openly enter a city, but had to remain outside, in deserted places. And they were gathered to him from every direction. (Mrk 1:45)

Hail Mary...

He departed again to the sea. And the entire crowd came to him, and he taught them. (Mrk 2:13)

Hail Mary...

A great crowd followed him from Galilee and Judea, and from Jerusalem, and from Idumea and across the Jordan. And those around Tyre and Sidon, upon hearing what he was doing, came to him in a great multitude. (Mrk 3:7-8)

Hail Mary...

He began to teach by the sea. A great crowd was gathered to him, so much so that, climbing into a boat on the sea, he sat there. And the entire crowd was on the land along the sea. And he taught them many things in parables. (Mrk 4:1-2)

Hail Mary...

Jesus, going out, saw a great multitude. And he took pity on them, because they were like sheep without a shepherd, and he began to teach them many things. (Mrk 6:34)

Hail Mary…

Rising up, he went from there to the area of Tyre and Sidon. And entering into a house, he intended no one to know about it, but he was not able to remain hidden. (Mrk 7:24)
Hail Mary…

He instructed them not to tell anyone. But as much as he instructed them, so much more did they preach about it. And so much more did they wonder, saying: "He has done all things well. He has caused both the deaf to hear and the mute to speak." (Mrk 7:36-37)
Hail Mary…

Rising up, he went from there into the area of Judea beyond the Jordan. And again, the crowd came together before him. And just as he was accustomed to do, again he taught them. (Mrk 10:1)
Hail Mary…

Arriving in his own country, he taught them in their synagogues, so much so that they wondered and said: "How can such wisdom and power be with this one?" (Matt 13:54)
Hail Mary…

Jesus returned, in the power of the Spirit, into Galilee. And his fame spread throughout the entire region. And he taught in their synagogues, and he was praised by everyone. (Luk 4:14-15)
Hail Mary…

Glory Be…

Decade 3
Our Father…

The Spirit of the Lord is upon me; because of this, he has anointed me. He has sent me to evangelize the poor, to heal the contrite of heart, to proclaim liberty to captives and sight to the blind, to let the oppressed go free, to preach the acceptable year of the Lord and the day of retribution. (Luk 4:18-19)
Hail Mary…

Everyone gave testimony to him. And they wondered at the words of grace that proceeded from his mouth. And they said, "Is this not the son of Joseph?" (Luk 4:22)
Hail Mary…

He descended to Capernaum, a city of Galilee. And there he taught them on the Sabbath. They were astonished at his teaching, for his word was spoken with authority. (Luk 4:31-32)
Hail Mary…

It happened that, when the crowds pressed toward him, so that they might hear the word of God, he was standing beside the lake of Genesaret. And he saw two boats standing beside the lake. But the fishermen had climbed down, and they were washing their nets. And so, climbing into one of the boats, which belonged to Simon, he asked him to draw back a little from the land. And sitting down, he taught the crowds from the boat. (Luk 5:1-3)
Hail Mary…

He was traveling through the cities and towns, teaching and making his way to Jerusalem. (Luk 13:22)
Hail Mary…

In the daytime, he was teaching in the temple. But truly, departing in the evening, he lodged on the mount that is called Olivet. And all the people arrived in the morning to listen to him in the temple. (Luk 21:37-38)
Hail Mary…

He said to them, "I must also preach the kingdom of God to other cities, because it was for this reason that I was sent." And he was preaching in the synagogues of Galilee. (Luk 4:43-44)
Hail Mary…

He was teaching in the temple daily. And the leaders of the priests, and the scribes, and the leaders of the people were seeking to destroy him. But they could not find what to do to him. For all the people were listening to him attentively. (Luk 19:47-48)
Hail Mary…

While he was at Jerusalem during the Passover, on the day of the feast, many believed in his name, seeing his signs that he was doing.(Jn 2:23)
Hail Mary…

After these things, Jesus and his disciples went into the land of Judea. And he was living there with them and baptizing. (Jn 3:22)
Hail Mary…

Glory Be…

Decade 4
Our Father…

Then, about the middle of the festival, Jesus ascended into the temple, and he was teaching. The Jews were astonished at it, saying: "How does this man have such learning, though he has not been taught?" (Jn 7:14-15)
Hail Mary…

Early in the morning, he went again to the temple; and all the people came to him. And sitting down, he taught them. (Jn 8:2)
Hail Mary…

He went again across the Jordan, to that place where John first was baptizing. And he lodged there. And many went out to him. And they were saying: "Indeed, John accomplished no signs. But everything that John said about this man were true." And many believed in him. (Jn 10:40-42)
Hail Mary…

Jesus also accomplished many other signs in the sight of his disciples. These have not been written in this book. But these things have been written, so that you may believe that Jesus is the Christ, the Son of God, and so that, in believing, you may have life in his name. (Jn 20:30-31)
Hail Mary…

There are also many other things that Jesus did, which, if each of these were written down, the world itself, I suppose, would not be able to contain the books that would be written. (Jn 21:25)
Hail Mary…

People of Israel, hear these words: Jesus the Nazarene is a man confirmed by God among you through the miracles and wonders and signs that God accomplished through him in your midst, just as you yourself know. (Acts 2:22)
Hail Mary…

When he had arrived in Galilee, the Galileans received him, because they had seen all that he had done at Jerusalem, in the day of the feast. For they also went to the feast day. (Jn 4:45)
Hail Mary…

I came into this world for judgment, so that those who do not see, may see; and so that those who see, may become blind. (Jn 9:39)
Hail Mary…

Jesus continued on to the Mount of Olives. And early in the morning, he went again to the temple; and all the people came to him. And sitting down, he taught them. (Jn 8:1-2)
Hail Mary…

There was a man among the Pharisees, named Nicodemus, a leader of the Jews. He went to Jesus at night, and he said to him: "Rabbi, we know that you have arrived as a teacher from God. For no one would be able to accomplish these signs, which you accomplish, unless God were with him." (Jn 3:1-2)
Hail Mary…

Glory Be…

Decade 5
Our Father…

His winnowing fork is in his hand. And he will thoroughly cleanse his threshing floor. And he will gather his wheat into the barn. But the chaff he will burn with unquenchable fire. (Matt 3:12)
Hail Mary…

The Son of man has come to seek and to save what had been lost. (Luk 19:10)
Hail Mary…

When the Samaritans had come to him, they petitioned him to lodge there. And he lodged there for two days. And many more believed in him, because of his own word. (Jn 4:40-41)
Hail Mary…

With many such parables he spoke the word to them, as much as they were able to hear. But he did not speak to them without a parable. (Mrk 4:33-34)
Hail Mary…

Jesus answered, "You are saying that I am a king. For this I was born, and for this I came into the world: so that I may offer testimony to the truth. Everyone who is of the truth hears my voice." (Jn 18:37)
Hail Mary…

I have made known your name to them, and I will make it known, so that the love in which you have loved me may be in them, and so that I may be in them. (Jn 17:26)
Hail Mary…

Jesus spoke in parables to the crowds. And he did not speak to them apart from parables, in order to fulfill what was spoken through the prophet, saying: "I will open my mouth in parables. I will proclaim what has been hidden since the foundation of the world." (Matt 13:34-35)
Hail Mary…

In that day, Jesus, departing from the house, sat down beside the sea. And such great crowds were gathered to him that he climbed into a boat and he sat down. And the entire multitude stood on the shore. And he spoke many things to them in parables. (Matt 13:1-3)
Hail Mary…

Behold, my servant whom I have chosen, my beloved in whom my soul is well pleased. I will place my Spirit over him, and he shall announce judgment to the nations. He shall not contend, nor cry out, neither shall anyone hear his voice in the streets. He shall not crush the bruised reed, and he shall not extinguish the smoking wick, until he sends forth judgment unto victory. And the Gentiles shall hope in his name. (Matt 12:18-21)
Hail Mary…

It happened that, when Jesus had completed instructing his twelve disciples, he went away from there in order to teach and to preach in their cities. (Matt 11:1)
Hail Mary…

Glory Be…

Healing and Deliverance Ministry of Jesus

Decade 1
Our Father…

His fame went throughout all Syria, and they brought to him all the sick people, those who were suffering from all kinds of diseases, pain, people with demons, epileptics, and paralytics, and he cured them. (Matt 4:24)
Hail Mary…

Behold, a leper, drawing near, adored him, saying, "Lord, if you are willing, you are able to cleanse me."And Jesus, extending his hand, touched him, saying: "I am willing. Be cleansed." And immediately his leprosy was cleansed. (Matt 8:2-3)
Hail Mary…

When evening arrived, they brought to him many who had demons, and he cast out the spirits with a word. And he healed all who were sick, in order to fulfill what was spoken through the prophet Isaiah, saying, "He took our infirmities, and he carried away our diseases." (Matt 8:16-17)
Hail Mary…

He then said to the paralytic, "Rise up, take up your bed, and go into your house." And he arose and went into his house. Then the crowd, seeing this, was frightened, and they glorified God, who gave such power to men. (Matt 9:6-8)
Hail Mary…

She said within herself, "If I will touch even his garment, I shall be saved." But Jesus, turning and seeing her, said: "Be strengthened in faith, daughter; your faith has made you well." And the woman was made well from that hour. (Matt 9:21-22)
Hail Mary…

When he had arrived at the house, the blind men approached him. And Jesus said to them, "Do you trust that I am able to do this for you?" They say to him, "Certainly, Lord." Then he touched their eyes, saying, "According to your faith, so let it be done for you." And their eyes were opened. (Matt 9:28-30)
Hail Mary…

Behold, they brought him a man who was mute, having a demon. And after the demon was cast out, the mute man spoke. And the crowds wondered, saying, "Never has anything like this been seen in Israel." (Matt 9:32-33)
Hail Mary...

Many crowds followed him, and he cured all of them. (Matt 12:15)
Hail Mary...

They brought to Jesus a man who was blind and mute because of a demon. Jesus healed him, so that he could speak and see (Matt 12:22)
Hail Mary...

The blind and the lame drew near to him in the temple; and he healed them. (Matt 21:14)
Hail Mary...

Glory Be...

Decade 2
Our Father...

Great crowds followed him, and he healed them there. (Matt 19:2)
Hail Mary...

Going out, he saw a great multitude, and he took pity on them, and he cured their sick. (Matt 14:14)
Hail Mary...

When the people of that place had recognized him, they sent into all that region, and they brought to him all the sick. And they petitioned him, so that they might touch even the hem of his garment. And as many as touched it were made well. (Matt 14:35-36)
Hail Mary...

Great multitudes came to him, having with them the mute, the blind, the lame, the disabled, and many others. And they cast them down at his feet, and he cured them. (Matt 15:30)
Hail Mary...

The people were amazed, seeing the mute speaking, the lame walking, the blind seeing. And they magnified the God of Israel. (Matt 15:31)
Hail Mary...

They say to him, "Lord, let our eyes be opened". Jesus had compassion on them and touched their eyes: and immediately they received their sight and followed him. (Matt 20:33-34)
Hail Mary...

They were all so amazed that they inquired among themselves, saying: "What is this? And what is this new teaching? For with authority he commands even the unclean spirits, and they obey him." (Mrk 1:27)
Hail Mary...

They went into the house of Simon and Andrew, with James and John. But the mother-in-law of Simon lay ill with a fever. And at once they told him about her. And drawing near to her, he raised her up, taking her by the hand. And immediately the fever left her, and she ministered to them. (Mrk 1:29-31)
Hail Mary...

When evening arrived, after the sun had set, they brought to him all who were sick or possessed with demons. And the entire city was gathered together at the door. And he healed many who were troubled with various illnesses. And he cast out many demons, but he would not permit them to speak, because they knew him. (Mrk 1:32-34)
Hail Mary...

He said to them: "Let us go into the neighboring towns and cities, so that I may preach there also. Indeed, it was for this reason that I came." And he was preaching in their synagogues and throughout all of Galilee, and casting out demons. (Mrk 1:38-39)
Hail Mary...

Glory Be...

Decade 3
Our Father...

It happened, on a certain day, that he again sat down, teaching. And there were Pharisees and teachers of the law sitting nearby, who had come from every town of Galilee and Judea and Jerusalem. And the power of the Lord was with him to heal. (Luk 5:17)
Hail Mary...

Jesus said to him, "What do you want me to do for you?" And the blind man said to him, "Master, let me see again." Then Jesus said to him, "Go, your faith has made you well." And immediately he saw, and he followed him on the way. (Mrk 10:51-52)

Hail Mary…

A leper came to him, begging him. And kneeling down, he said to him, "If you choose, you can make me clean." Then Jesus, taking pity on him, reached out his hand. And touching him, he said to him: "I do choose. Be made clean! " And after he had spoken, immediately the leprosy departed from him, and he was cleansed. (Mrk 1:40-42)
Hail Mary…

He healed so many, that as many of them as had diseases would rush toward him in order to touch him. And the unclean spirits, when they saw him, fell prostrate before him. And they cried out, saying, "You are the Son of God." And he sternly ordered them not to make him known. (Mrk 3:10-12)
Hail Mary…

When she had heard of Jesus, she approached through the crowd behind him, and she touched his garment. For she said: "Because if I touch even his garment, I will be saved." And immediately, the source of her bleeding was dried up, and she sensed in her body that she had been healed from the wound. (Mrk 5:27-29)
Hail Mary...

He said to her: "Daughter, your faith has saved you. Go in peace, and be healed from your wound." (Mrk 5:34)
Hail Mary...

When they had disembarked from the boat, the people immediately recognized him. And running throughout that entire region, they began to carry on beds those who were sick, to whereever they heard that he would be. (Mrk 6:54-55)
Hail Mary…

In whichever place he entered, in towns or villages or cities, they placed the infirm in the main streets, and they pleaded with him that they might touch even the hem of his garment. And as many as touched him were made healthy. (Mrk 6:56)
Hail Mary...

They brought someone who was deaf and mute to him. And they begged him, so that he would lay his hand upon him. And taking him away from the crowd, he put his fingers into his ears; and spitting, he touched his tongue. And gazing up to heaven, he groaned and said to him: "Ephphatha," which is, "Be opened." And immediately his ears were opened, and the impediment of his tongue was released, and he spoke correctly. (Mrk 7:32-35)

Hail Mary…

When Jesus saw the crowd rushing together, he rebuked the unclean spirit, saying to him, "Deaf and mute spirit, I command you, leave him; and do not enter into him anymore." And crying out, and convulsing him greatly, he departed from him. And he became like one who is dead, so much so that many said, "He is dead." But Jesus, taking him by the hand, lifted him up. And he arose. (Mrk 9:25-27)
Hail Mary…

Glory Be…

Decade 4
Our Father…

In the synagogue, there was a man who had an unclean demon, and he cried out with a loud voice, saying: "Let us alone. What are we to you, Jesus of Nazareth? Have you come to destroy us? I know who you are: the Holy One of God." And Jesus rebuked him, saying, "Be silent and depart from him." And when the demon had thrown him into their midst, he departed from him, and he no longer harmed him. (Luk 4:33-35)
Hail Mary...

Word about Jesus spread all the more widely, And great crowds came together, so that they might listen and be cured by him from their diseases. (Luk 5:15)
Hail Mary...

They had come so that they might listen to him and be healed of their diseases. And those who were troubled by unclean spirits were cured. (Luk 6:18)
Hail Mary...

The entire crowd was trying to touch him, because power went out from him and healed all. (Luk 6:19)
Hail Mary...

Fear fell over them all. And they discussed this among themselves, saying: "What is this word? For with authority and power he commands the unclean spirits, and they depart." (Luk 4:36)
Hail Mary…

When the sun had set, all those who had anyone afflicted with various diseases brought them to him. Then, laying his hands on each one of them, he cured them. (Luk 4:40)

Hail Mary…

Demons departed from many of them, crying out and saying, "You are the son of God." And rebuking them, he would not permit them to speak. For they knew him to be the Christ. (Luk 4:41)
Hail Mary…

It happened that, while he was in a certain city, behold, there was a man full of leprosy who, upon seeing Jesus and falling to his face, petitioned him, saying: "Lord, if you are willing, you are able to cleanse me." And extending his hand, he touched him, saying: "I am willing. Be cleansed." And at once, the leprosy departed from him. (Luk 5:12-13)
Hail Mary…

He said to the paralytic, "I say to you to: Rise up, take up your bed, and go into your house."And at once, rising up in their sight, he took up the bed on which he was lying, and he went away to his own house, magnifying God. (Luk 5:24-25)
Hail Mary…

It was the power of his name that has given this man complete health in the sight of you all. And by faith in Jesus, this man, whom you have seen and known, has been made well. (Acts 3:16)
Hail Mary...

Glory Be…

Decade 5
Our Father…

Let it be known to all of you and to all of the people of Israel, that in the name of our Lord Jesus Christ the Nazarene, whom you crucified, whom God has raised from the dead, by him, this man stands before you, healthy. (Acts 4:10)
Hail Mary…

He found there a certain man, named Aeneas, who was a paralytic, who had lain in bed for eight years. And Peter said to him: "Aeneas, the Lord Jesus Christ heals you. Rise up and arrange your bed." And immediately he rose up. (Acts 9:33-34)
Hail Mary…

Jesus of Nazareth, whom God anointed with the Holy Spirit and with power, traveled around doing good and healing all those oppressed by the devil. For God was with him. (Acts 10:38)
Hail Mary...

He spat on the ground, and he made clay from the spittle, and he smeared the clay over his eyes. And he said to him: "Go, wash in the pool of Siloam". Therefore, he went away and washed, and he came back able to see. (Jn 9:6-7)
Hail Mary…

As he was entering a certain town, ten leprous men met him, and they stood at a distance. And they lifted up their voice, saying, "Jesus, Teacher, take pity on us." And when he saw them, he said, "Go, show yourselves to the priests." And it happened that, as they were going, they were cleansed. (Luk 17:12-14)
Hail Mary…

Jesus, standing still, ordered him to be brought to him. And when he had drawn near, he questioned him, saying, "What do you want, that I might do for you?" So he said, "Lord, that I may see." And Jesus said to him: "Receive your sight; Your faith has saved you." And immediately he saw. And he followed him, glorifying God. (Luk 18:40-43)
Hail Mary…

He was casting out a demon, and the man was mute. But when he had cast out the demon, the mute man spoke, and so the crowds were amazed. (Luk 11:14)
Hail Mary…

When John had heard, in prison, about the works of Christ, sending two of his disciples, he said to him, "Are you he who is to come, or should we expect another?" And Jesus, responding, said to them: "Go and report to John what you have heard and seen. The blind see, the lame walk, the lepers are cleansed, the deaf hear, the dead rise again, the poor are evangelized. And blessed is he who has found no offense in me." (Matt 11:2-6)
Hail Mary…

The centurion said: "Lord, I am not worthy that you should enter under my roof, but only say the word, and my servant shall be healed. (Matt 8:8)
Hail Mary…

Jesus said to them: "This sickness is not unto death, but for the glory of God, so that the Son of God may be glorified by it." (Jn 11:4)
Hail Mary…

Glory Be…

Beatitudes and the Sermon on the Mount

Decade 1
Our Father…

Blessed are the poor in spirit, for theirs is the kingdom of heaven. (Matt 5:3)
Hail Mary…

Blessed are the meek, for they shall possess the earth. (Matt 5:4)
Hail Mary…

Blessed are those who mourn, for they shall be consoled. (Matt 5:5)
Hail Mary…

Blessed are those who hunger and thirst for justice, for they shall be satisfied. (Matt 5:6)
Hail Mary…

Blessed are the merciful, for they shall obtain mercy. (Matt 5:7)
Hail Mary…

Blessed are the pure in heart, for they shall see God. (Matt 5:8)
Hail Mary…

Blessed are the peacemakers, for they shall be called children of God. (Matt 5:9)
Hail Mary…

Blessed are those who endure persecution for the sake of justice, for theirs is the kingdom of heaven. (Matt 5:10)
Hail Mary…

Blessed are you when they have slandered you, and persecuted you, and spoken all kinds of evil against you, falsely, for my sake: be glad and exult, for your reward in heaven is plentiful. For so they persecuted the prophets who were before you. (Matt 5:11-12)
Hail Mary…

You are the salt of the earth. But if salt loses its saltiness, with what will it be salted? It is no longer useful at all, except to be cast out and trampled under by men. (Matt 5:13)
Hail Mary…

Decade 2
Our Father…

You are the light of the world. A city set on a mountain cannot be hidden. No one lights a lamp and put it under a bushel basket, but on a lampstand, so that it may shine to all who are in the house. (Matt 5:14-15)
Hail Mary…

Let your light shine in the sight of men, so that they may see your good works, and may glorify your Father, who is in heaven. (Matt 5:16)
Hail Mary…

Do not think that I have come to abolish the law or the prophets. I have not come to abolish, but to fulfill. Amen I say to you, certainly, until heaven and earth pass away, not one stroke of a letter shall pass away from the law, until all is done. (Matt 5:17-18)
Hail Mary…

Therefore, whoever breaks one of the least of these commandments, and teaches others to do the same, shall be called the least in the kingdom of heaven. But whoever does them and teaches them shall be called great in the kingdom of heaven. (Matt 5:19)
Hail Mary…

Unless your righteousness has surpassed that of the scribes and the Pharisees you shall not enter into the kingdom of heaven. (Matt 5:20)
Hail Mary…

You have heard that it was said to the ancients: 'You shall not murder; whoever will have murdered shall be liable to judgment.'But I say to you, that anyone who becomes angry with his brother or sister shall be liable to judgment. But whoever will have insulted his brother or sister shall be liable to the council. Then, whoever will have called him, 'you fool,' shall be liable to the fires of Hell. (Matt 5:21-22)
Hail Mary…

If you offer your gift at the altar, and there you remember that your brother has something against you, leave your gift there, before the altar, and go first to be reconciled to your brother, and then you may approach and offer your gift. (Matt 5:23-24)
Hail Mary…

Be reconciled with your adversary quickly, while you are still on the way with him, lest perhaps the adversary may hand you over to the judge, and the judge may hand you over to the officer, and you will be thrown in prison. Amen I say to you, that you shall not go forth from there, until you have repaid the last quarter. (Matt 5:25-26)
Hail Mary…

You have heard that it was said to the ancients: 'You shall not commit adultery.' But I say to you, that anyone who will have looked at a woman, so as to lust after her, has already committed adultery with her in his heart. (Matt 5:27-28)
Hail Mary…

And if your right eye causes you to sin, root it out and cast it away from you. For it is better for you that one of your members perish, than that your whole body be cast into Hell. And if your right hand causes you to sin, cut it off and cast it away from you. For it is better for you that one of your members perish, than that your whole body go into Hell. (Matt 5:29-30)
Hail Mary…

Glory Be…

Decade 3
Our Father…

It has been said: 'Whoever would dismiss his wife, let him give her a bill of divorce.'But I say to you, that anyone who will have dismissed his wife, except in the case of fornication, causes her to commit adultery; and whoever will have married her who has been dismissed commits adultery. (Matt 5:31-32)
Hail Mary…

You have heard that it was said to the ancients: 'You shall not swear falsely. For you shall repay your oaths to the Lord.' But I say to you, do not swear an oath at all, neither by heaven, for it is the throne of God, nor by earth, for it is his footstool, nor by Jerusalem, for it is the city of the great king. Neither shall you swear an oath by your own head, because you are not able to cause one hair to become white or black. But let your word 'Yes' mean 'Yes,' and 'No' mean 'No.' For anything beyond that is of evil. (Matt 5:33-37)
Hail Mary…

You have heard that it was said: 'An eye for an eye, and a tooth for a tooth.' But I say to you, do not resist one who is evil, but if anyone will have struck you on your right cheek, offer to him the other also. (Matt 5:38-39)
Hail Mary…

Anyone who wishes to contend with you in judgment, and to take away your tunic, release to him your cloak also. And whoever will have compelled you for one thousand steps, go with him even for two thousand steps. Whoever asks of you, give to him. And if anyone would borrow from you, do not turn away from him. (Matt 5:40-42)
Hail Mary…

You have heard that it was said, 'You shall love your neighbor, and you shall have hatred for your enemy.' But I say to you: Love your enemies. Do good to those who hate you. And pray for those who persecute and slander you, So that you may be children of your Father, who is in heaven. He causes his sun to rise upon the good and the bad, and he causes it to rain upon the just and the unjust. (Matt 5:43-45)
Hail Mary…

If you love those who love you, what reward will you have? Do not even tax collectors behave this way? And if you greet only your brothers, what more have you done? Do not even the pagans behave this way? Therefore, be perfect, even as your heavenly Father is perfect." (Matt 5:46-48)
Hail Mary…

Watch out, Don't perform your good deeds publicly, in order to be seen by others; otherwise you will lose the reward from your Father, who is in heaven. (Matt 6:1)
Hail Mary…

When you give alms, do not choose to sound a trumpet before you, as the hypocrites do in the synagogues and in the towns, so that they may be honored by men. Amen I say to you, they have received their reward. But when you give alms, do not let your left hand know what your right hand is doing, so that your almsgiving may be in secret, and your Father, who sees in secret, will repay you. (Matt 6:1-4)
Hail Mary…

When you pray, you should not be like the hypocrites, who love standing in the synagogues and at the corners of the streets to pray, so that they may be seen by men. Amen I say to you, they have received their reward. But you, when you pray, enter into your room, and having shut the door, pray to your Father in secret, and your Father, who sees in secret, will repay you. (Matt 6:5-6)
Hail Mary…

When praying, do not choose many words, as the pagans do. For they think that by their excess of words they might be heard. Therefore, do not choose

to imitate them. For your Father knows what your needs may be, even before you ask him. (Matt 6:7-8)
Hail Mary…

Glory Be…

Decade 4
Our Father…

Therefore, you shall pray in this way: Our Father in heaven: Holy be your name. Your kingdom come. Your will be done on Earth, as it is in heaven. Give us this day our daily bread. And forgive us our debts, as we also forgive our debtors. And lead us not into temptation. But deliver us from evil. Amen. (Matt 6:9-13)
Hail Mary…

For if you will forgive men their sins, your heavenly Father also will forgive you your offenses. But if you will not forgive men, neither will your Father forgive you your sins. (Matt 6:14-15)
Hail Mary…

When you fast, do not choose to become gloomy, like the hypocrites. For they alter their faces, so that their fasting may be apparent to men. Amen I say to you, that they have received their reward. But as for you, when you fast, anoint your head and wash your face, so that your fasting will not be apparent to men, but to your Father, who is in secret. And your Father, who sees in secret, will repay you. (Matt 6:16-18)
Hail Mary…

Do not choose to store up for yourselves treasures on earth: where rust and moth consume, and where thieves break in and steal. Instead, store up for yourselves treasures in heaven: where neither rust nor moth consumes, and where thieves do not break in and steal. For where your treasure is, there also is your heart. (Matt 6:19-21)
Hail Mary…

The lamp of your body is your eye. If your eye is wholesome, your entire body will be filled with light. But if your eye has been corrupted, your entire body will be darkened. If then the light that is in you is darkness, how great will that darkness be! (Matt 6:22-23)
Hail Mary…

No one is able to serve two masters. For either he will have hatred for the one, and love the other, or he will persevere with the one, and despise the other. You cannot serve God and wealth. (Matt 6:24)

Hail Mary...

Do not worry about your life, as to what you will eat, nor about your body, as to what you will wear. Is not life more than food, and the body more than clothing? (Matt 6:25)
Hail Mary...

Consider the birds of the air, how they neither sow, nor reap, nor gather into barns, and yet your heavenly Father feeds them. Are you not of much greater value than they are? (Matt 6:26)
Hail Mary...

Which of you, by worrying, is able to add single hour to your span of life? And why do you worry about clothing? Consider the lilies of the field, how they grow; they neither work nor weave. But I say to you, that not even Solomon, in all his glory, was clothed like one of these. So if God so clothes the grass of the field, which is here today, and cast into the oven tomorrow, how much more will clothe you, O little in faith? (Matt 6:27-30)
Hail Mary...

Therefore, do not worry, saying: 'What shall we eat, and what shall we drink, and with what shall we be clothed?' For the Gentiles seek all these things. Yet your Father knows that you need all these things. (Matt 6:31-32)
Hail Mary...

Glory Be...

Decade 5
Our Father...

Seek first the kingdom of God and his righteousness, and all these things shall be added to you as well. Therefore, do worry about tomorrow; for the future day will bring worries of its own. Todays trouble is enough for the day. (Matt 6:33-34)
Hail Mary...

Do not judge, so that you may not be judged. For with whatever judgment you judge, so shall you be judged; and with whatever measure you measure out, so shall it be measured back to you. (Matt 7:1-2)
Hail Mary...

And how can you see the splinter in your brother's eye, and not see the log in your own eye? Or how can you say to your brother, 'Let me take the splinter from your eye,' while, behold, a board is in your own eye?

Hypocrite, first remove the log from your own eye, and then you will see clearly enough to remove the splinter from your brother's eye. (Matt 7:3-5)
Hail Mary…

Do not give what is holy to dogs, and do not cast your pearls before swine, lest perhaps they may trample them under their feet, and then, turning, they may tear you apart. (Matt 7:7)
Hail Mary…

Ask, and it shall be given to you. Seek, and you shall find. Knock, and it shall be opened to you. For everyone who asks, receives; and whoever seeks, finds; and to anyone who knocks, it will be opened. (Matt 7:7-8)
Hail Mary…

Or what man is there among you, who, if his son were to ask him for bread, would offer him a stone; or if he were to ask him for a fish, would offer him a snake? Therefore, if you, though you are evil, know how to give good gifts to your children, how much more will your Father, who is in heaven, give good things to those who ask him? (Matt 7:9-11)
Hail Mary…

In all things whatever that you wish that others would do to you, do so also to them. For this is the law and the prophets. (Matt 7:12)
Hail Mary…

Enter through the narrow gate. For wide is the gate, and broad is the way, which leads to destruction, and many there are who enter through it. But the gate to life is narrow and the way that leads to it is hard, and there are few people who find it. (Matt 7:13-14)
Hail Mary…

Beware of false prophets, who come to you in sheep's clothing, but inwardly are ravenous wolves. You shall know them by their fruits. Can grapes be gathered from thorns, or figs from thistles? (Matt 7:15-16)
Hail Mary…

So then, every good tree produces good fruit, and the evil tree produces evil fruit. A good tree is not able to produce evil fruit, and an evil tree is not able to produce good fruit. Every tree which does not produce good fruit shall be cut down and cast into the fire. Therefore, by their fruits you will know them. (Matt 7:17-20)
Hail Mary…

Glory Be…

Words of Jesus (Gospel of Matthew)

Decade 1
Our Father…

Not all who say to me, 'Lord, Lord,' will enter into the kingdom of heaven. But whoever does the will of my Father, who is in heaven, the same shall enter into the kingdom of heaven. (Matt 7:21)
Hail Mary…

Many will say to me in that day, 'Lord, Lord, did we not prophesy in your name, and cast out demons in your name, and perform many powerful deeds in your name?' And then will I disclose to them: 'I have never known you. Depart from me, you workers of iniquity.' (Matt 7:22-23)
Hail Mary…

Everyone who hears these words of mine and does them shall be compared to a wise man, who built his house upon the rock. And the rains descended, and the floods rose up, and the winds blew, and rushed upon that house, but it did not fall, for it was founded on the rock. (Matt 7:24-25)
Hail Mary…

Everyone who hears these words of mine and does not do them shall be like a foolish man, who built his house upon the sand. And the rains descended, and the floods rose up, and the winds blew, and rushed upon that house, and it did fall, and great was its ruin." (Matt 7:26-27)
Hail Mary…

I say to you, that many shall come from the east and the west, and they shall sit at table with Abraham, and Isaac, and Jacob in the kingdom of heaven. But the heirs of the kingdom shall be cast into the outer darkness, where there will be weeping and gnashing of teeth. (Matt 8:11-12)
Hail Mary…

One scribe, approaching, said to him, "Teacher, I will follow you wherever you will go." And Jesus said to him, "Foxes have dens, and the birds of the air have nests, but the Son of man has nowhere to rest his head." (Matt 8:19-20)
Hail Mary…

Another of his disciples said to him, "Lord, permit me first to go and bury my father." But Jesus said to him, "Follow me, and allow the dead to bury their dead." (Matt 8:21-22)

Hail Mary…

It is not those who are healthy who are in need of a physician, but those who who are sick. So then, go out and learn what this means: 'I desire mercy and not sacrifice.' For I have not come to call the righteous, but sinners." (Matt 9:12-13)
Hail Mary…

No one would sew a patch of new cloth onto an old garment. For it pulls its fullness away from the garment, and the tear is made worse. Neither do they pour new wine into old wineskins. Otherwise, the wineskins rupture, and the wine pours out, and the wineskins are destroyed. Instead, they pour new wine into new wineskins. And so, both are preserved. (Mrk 9:16-17)
Hail Mary…

The harvest indeed is great, but the laborers are few. Therefore, petition the Lord of the harvest, so that he may send out laborers to his harvest. (Matt 9:37-38)
Hail Mary…

Glory Be…

Decade 2
Our Father…

Do not be afraid of those who kill the body, but are not able to kill the soul. But instead fear him who is able to destroy both soul and body in Hell. (Matt 10:28)
Hail Mary...

Are not two sparrows sold for one small coin? And yet not one of them will fall to the ground apart from your Father. For even the hairs of your head have all been numbered. Therefore, do not be afraid. You are worth more than many sparrows. (Matt 10:29-31)
Hail Mary...

Everyone who acknowledges me before men, I also will acknowledge before my Father, who is in heaven. But whoever will have denied me before men, I also will deny before my Father, who is in heaven. (Matt 10:32-33)
Hail Mary...

Do not think that I came to bring peace upon the earth. I came, not to bring peace, but the sword. For I came to divide a man against his father, and a daughter against her mother, and a daughter-in-law against her mother-in-law. And the enemies of a man will be those of his own household. (Matt 10:34-36)

Hail Mary...

Whoever loves father or mother more than me is not worthy of me. And whoever loves son or daughter above me is not worthy of me. And whoever does not take up his cross and follow me is not worthy of me. (Matt 10:37-38)

Hail Mary...

Whoever receives you, receives me. And whoever receives me, receives him who sent me. Whoever receives a prophet, in the name of a prophet, shall receive the reward of a prophet. And whoever receives the just in the name of the just shall receive the reward of the just. And whoever shall give, even to one of the least of these, a cup of cold water to drink, solely in the name of a disciple: Amen I say to you, he shall not lose his reward. (Matt 10:40-42)

Hail Mary…

Come to me, all you who labor and have been burdened, and I will give you rest. (Matt 11:28)

Hail Mary...

Take my yoke upon you, and learn from me, for I am meek and humble of heart; and you shall find rest for your souls. For my yoke is easy and my burden is light. (Matt 11:29-30)

Hail Mary...

Who is there among you, having only one sheep, if it will have fallen into a pit on the Sabbath, would not take hold of it and lift it up? How much more valuable is a man than a sheep? And so, it is lawful to do good on the Sabbath. (Matt 12:11-12)

Hail Mary…

Whoever is not with me, is against me. And whoever does not gather with me, scatters. (Matt 12:30)

Hail Mary...

Glory Be…

Decade 3

Our Father…

Either make the tree good and its fruit good, or make the tree evil and its fruit evil. For a tree is known by its fruit. (Matt 12:33)

Hail Mary…

How are you able to speak good things while you are evil? For out of the abundance of the heart, the mouth speaks. A good person brings good things from a good treasure. And an evil person brings evil things from an evil treasure. (Matt 12:34-35)
Hail Mary…

For every idle word which men will have spoken, they shall render an account in the day of judgment. For by your words shall you be justified, and by your words shall you be condemned. (Matt 12:36-37)
Hail Mary…

Anyone who does the will of my Father, who is in heaven is my brother, and sister, and mother. (Matt 12:50)
Hail Mary…

The kingdom of heaven is like a treasure hidden in a field. When a man finds it, he hides it, and, because of his joy, he goes and sells everything that he has, and he buys that field. (Matt 13:44)
Hail Mary…

The kingdom of heaven is like a merchant seeking good pearls. Having found one pearl of great value, he went away and sold all that he had, and he bought it. (Matt 13:45-46)
Hail Mary…

If anyone is willing to come after me, let him deny himself, and take up his cross, and follow me. (Matt 16:24)
Hail Mary...

Even if you have faith as small as a mustard seed, you could say to this mountain, 'move from here to there', and it shall move; and nothing will be impossible for you. (Matt 17:20)
Hail Mary…

Whoever will have led astray one of these little ones, who trust in me, it would be better for him to have a great millstone hung around his neck, and to be submerged in the depths of the sea. (Matt 18:6)
Hail Mary...

If your hand or your foot leads you to sin, cut it off and cast it away from you. It is better for you to enter into life disabled or lame, than to be sent into eternal fire having two hands or two feet. (Matt 18:8)
Hail Mary...

Glory Be…

Decade 4

Our Father…

If your eye leads you to sin, root it out and cast it away from you. It is better for you to enter into life with one eye, than to be sent into the fires of Hell having two eyes. (Matt 18:9)
Hail Mary…

If someone has one hundred sheep, and if one of them has gone astray, should he not leave behind the ninety-nine in the mountains, and go out to seek what has gone astray? And if he should happen to find it: Amen I say to you, that he has more joy over that one, than over the ninety-nine which did not go astray. Even so, it is not the will before your Father, who is in heaven, that one of these little ones should be lost. (Matt 18:12-14)
Hail Mary…

If two of you have agreed on earth, about anything you ask, it shall be done for you by my Father, who is in heaven. For wherever two or three are gathered in my name, there am I, in their midst. (Matt 18:19-20)
Hail Mary…

Peter came and said to him, "Lord, if another member of the church sins against me, how often should I forgive? As many as seven times?" Jesus said to him, "Not seven times, but, I tell you, seventy-seven times." (Matt 18:21-22)
Hail Mary…

Allow the little children to come to me, and do not choose to prohibit them. For the kingdom of heaven is among such as these. (Matt 19:14)
Hail Mary…

If you are willing to be perfect, go, sell what you have, and give to the poor, and then you will have treasure in heaven. And come, follow me. (Matt 19:21)
Hail Mary…

For men, it is impossible. But for God, all things are possible. (Matt 19:26)
Hail Mary…

Anyone who has left behind home, or brothers, or sisters, or father, or mother, or wife, or children, or land, for the sake of my name, shall receive one hundred times more, and shall possess eternal life. But many of those who are first shall be last, and the last shall be first. (Matt 19:29-30)
Hail Mary…

Whoever will want to be greater among you, let him be your servant. And whoever will want to be first among you, he shall be your slave, just as the Son of man has not come to be served, but to serve, and to give his life as a ransom for many. (Matt 20:26-28)
Hail Mary...

'You shall love the Lord your God from all your heart, and with all your soul and with all your mind.' This is the greatest and first commandment. But the second is similar to it: 'You shall love your neighbor as yourself.' On these two commandments the entire law depends, and also the prophets. (Matt 22:37-40)
Hail Mary...

Glory Be...

Decade 5
Our Father...

He who is greatest among you will be your servant. (Matt 23:11)
Hail Mary...

Whoever has exalted himself, shall be humbled. And whoever has humbled himself, shall be exalted. (Matt 23:12)
Hail Mary...

Pay attention, lest someone lead you astray. For many will come in my name saying, 'I am the Christ.' And they will lead many astray. For you will hear of battles and rumors of battles. Take care not to be disturbed. For these things must be, but the end is not so soon. (Matt 24:4-6)
Hail Mary...

Nation will rise against nation, and kingdom against kingdom. And there will be pestilences, and famines, and earthquakes in places. But all these things are just the beginning of the sorrows. Then they will hand you over to tribulation, and they will kill you. And you will be hated by all nations for the sake of my name. And then many will be led into sin, and will betray one another, and will have hatred for one another. (Matt 24:7-10)
Hail Mary...

Many false prophets will arise, and they will lead many astray. And because iniquity has abounded, the love of many will grow cold. But whoever will have persevered until the end, the same shall be saved. (Matt 24:11-13)
Hail Mary...

Amen, I say to you, if you have faith, and do not doubt, not only will you do what has been done to this fig tree, but also if you will say to this mountain, 'be lifted up and be thrown into the sea,' it will be done. (Matt 21:21)
Hail Mary…

In all things whatever you shall ask for in prayer with faith, you shall receive. (Matt 21:22)
Hail Mary…

Immediately after the tribulation of those days, the sun will be darkened, and the moon will not give its light, and the stars will fall from heaven, and the powers of the heavens will be shaken. And then the sign of the Son of man shall appear in heaven. And then all tribes of the earth shall mourn. And they shall see the Son of man coming on the clouds of heaven, with great power and majesty. (Matt 24:29-30)
Hail Mary…

For to everyone who has, more shall be given, and he shall have in abundance. But from him who has not, even what he seems to have, shall be taken away. (Matt 25:29)
Hail Mary…

Stay awake and pray, so that you may not enter into the time of trial. Indeed, the spirit is willing, but the flesh is weak." (Matt 26:41)
Hail Mary…

Glory Be…

Words of Jesus (Gospel of Mark)

Decade 1
Our Father…

The time has been fulfilled and the kingdom of God has drawn near. Repent and believe in the Gospel. (Mrk 1:15)
Hail Mary...

No one sews a patch of new cloth onto an old garment. Otherwise, the new addition pulls away from the old, and the tear becomes worse. And no one puts new wine into old wineskins. Otherwise, the wine will burst the wineskins, and the wine will pour out, and the wineskins will be lost. Instead, new wine must be put into new wineskins. (Mrk 2:21-22)
Hail Mary...

The Sabbath was made for man, and not man for the Sabbath. And so, the Son of man is Lord, even of the Sabbath. (Mrk 2:27-28)
Hail Mary...

For whoever has done the will of God, the same is my brother, and my sister and mother. (Mrk 3:35)
Hail Mary...

To you, it has been given to know the mystery of the kingdom of God. But to those who are outside, everything is presented in parables: so that, they may indeed look, but not perceive; and may indeed hear, but not understand; so that they may not turn again and be forgiven. (Mrk 4:11-12)
Hail Mary…

Pay attention to what you hear; the measure you give will be the measure you get, and still more will be given you. (Mrk 4:24)
Hail Mary…

For whoever has, to him it shall be given more. And whoever has not, from him even what he has shall be taken away. (Mrk 4:25)
Hail Mary...

To what should we compare the kingdom of God? Or to what parable should we compare it? It is like a grain of mustard seed which, when it has been sown in the earth, is less than all the seeds which are in the earth. And when it is sown, it grows up and becomes greater than all the plants, and it

produces great branches, so much so that the birds of the air are able to live under its shadow. (Mrk 4:30-32)
Hail Mary…

Go to your own people, in your own house, and announce to them how great are the things that the Lord has done for you, and how he has taken pity on you. (Mrk 5:19)
Hail Mary…

A prophet is not without honor, except in his own country, and in his own house, and among his own kindred. (Mrk 6:4)
Hail Mary…

Glory Be…

Decade 2
Our Father…

Listen to me, all of you, and understand. There is nothing from outside a man which, by entering into him, is able to defile him. But the things which proceed from a man, these are what defile a man. (Mrk 7:14-15)
Hail Mary…

For from within, from the heart of men, come evil thoughts which lead you to do immoral things, to rob, kill, commit adultery, be greedy, and do all sorts of evil things; deceit, fornication, envy, slander, pride, and folly — all these evil things come from inside you and make you unclean. (Mrk 7:21-23)
Hail Mary…

Why does this generation seek a sign? Amen, I say to you, no sign will be given to this generation. (Mrk 8:12)
Hail Mary…

If anyone chooses to follow me, let him deny himself, and take up his cross, and follow me. (Mrk 8:34)
Hail Mary…

For whoever will have chosen to save his life, will lose it. But whoever will have lost his life, for my sake and for the Gospel, shall save it. (Mrk 8:35)
Hail Mary…

What shall it profit a man, if he gain the whole world, and suffer the loss of his soul? Or what shall a man give in exchange for his soul? (Mrk 8:36-37)
Hail Mary…

Whoever has been ashamed of me and of my words, among this adulterous and sinful generation, the Son of man also will be ashamed of him, when he will arrive in the glory of his Father, with the holy Angels. (Mrk 8:38)
Hail Mary…

Amen I say to you, that there are some among those standing here who shall not taste death until they see the kingdom of God arriving in power. (Mrk 9:1)
Hail Mary…

If you are able to believe: all things are possible to one who believes. (Mrk 9:23)
Hail Mary...

If anyone wants to be first, he shall be the last of all and the servant of all. (Mrk 9:35)
Hail Mary…

Glory Be…

Decade 3
Our Father…

Taking a child, he set him in their midst. And when he had embraced him, he said to them: "Whoever receives one such child in my name, receives me. And whoever receives me, receives not me, but him who sent me." (Mrk 9:36-37)
Hail Mary…

There is no one who does a deed of power in my name and soon speak evil about me. For whoever is not against you is for you. (Mrk 9:39-40)
Hail Mary…

Whoever will give you a cup of water to drink, because you bear the name of Christ: Amen I say to you, he shall not lose his reward. (Mrk 9:41)
Hail Mary…

If any of you put a stumbling block before one of these little ones who believe in me: it would be better for him if a great millstone were placed around his neck and he were thrown into the sea. (Mrk 9:42)
Hail Mary…

If your hand causes you to sin, cut it off: it is better for you to enter into life disabled, than having two hands to go into Hell, into the unquenchable fire. If your foot causes you to sin, chop it off: it is better for you to enter into

eternal life lame, than having two feet to be cast into the Hell of unquenchable fire. (Mrk 9:43-45)
Hail Mary…

If your eye causes you to sin, pluck it out: it is better for you to enter into the kingdom of God with one eye, than having two eyes to be cast into the Hell of fire, where their worm does not die, and the fire is not extinguished. (Mrk 9:47-48)
Hail Mary…

All shall be salted with fire, and every victim shall be salted with salt. Salt is good: but if the salt has lost its saltiness, with what will you season it? Have salt in yourselves, and have peace among yourselves. (Mrk 9:49-50)
Hail Mary…

From the beginning of creation, God made them male and female. Because of this, a man shall leave behind his father and mother, and he shall cling to his wife. And these two shall be one in flesh. And so, they are now, not two, but one flesh. Therefore, what God has joined together, let no man separate. (Mrk 10:6-9)
Hail Mary…

Whoever divorces his wife, and marries another, commits adultery against her. And if a wife divorces her husband, and is married to another, she commits adultery. (Mrk 10:11-12)
Hail Mary…

Allow the little ones to come to me, and do not prohibit them. For of such as these is the kingdom of God. Amen I say to you, whoever will not accept the kingdom of God like a little child, will not enter into it. (Mrk 10:14-15)
Hail Mary...

Glory Be…

Decade 4
Our Father…

It is easier for a camel to pass through the eye of a needle, than for the rich to enter into the kingdom of God. (Mrk 10:25)
Hail Mary...

Amen I say to you, There is no one who has left behind house, or brothers, or sisters, or father, or mother, or children, or land, for my sake and for the Gospel, who will not receive one hundred times as much, now in this time:

houses, and brothers, and sisters, and mothers, and children, and land, with persecutions, and in the future age eternal life. (Mrk 10:29-30)
Hail Mary...

You know that those who are leaders among the Gentiles rule over them, and their leaders exercise authority over them. But it is not to be this way among you. Instead, whoever would become greater shall be your servant; and whoever will be first among you shall be the servant of all. (Mrk 10:42-44)
Hail Mary...

The Son of Man came not to be served but to serve, and to give his life a ransom for many. (Mrk 10:45)
Hail Mary...

Amen I say to you, that whoever will say to this mountain, 'Be taken up and cast into the sea,' and who will not have hesitated in his heart, but will have believed: then whatever he has said be done, it shall be done for him. (Mrk 11:23)
Hail Mary...

All things whatever you ask for when praying, believe that you have received them, and they will be yours. (Mrk 11:24)
Hail Mary...

When you stand to pray, if you hold anything against anyone, forgive them, so that your Father, who is in heaven, may also forgive you your sins. But if you will not forgive, neither will your Father, who is in heaven, forgive you your sins. (Mrk 11:25-26)
Hail Mary...

Give to Caesar, the things that are of Caesar; and to God, the things that are of God. (Mrk 12:17)
Hail Mary…

You must love the Lord your God with all your heart, and with all your soul, and with all your mind, and with all your strength; and you must love your neighbor as you love yourself. It is more important to obey these two commandments than to offer on the altar animals and other sacrifices to God. (Mrk 12:33)
Hail Mary…

Concerning the dead who rise again, have you not read in the book of Moses, how God spoke to him from the bush, saying: 'I am the God of Abraham,

and the God of Isaac, and the God of Jacob?' He is not the God of the dead, but of the living. (Mrk 12:26-27)
Hail Mary…

Glory Be…

Decade 5
Our Father…

The first commandment of all is this: 'Listen, O Israel. The Lord your God is one God. And you shall love the Lord your God from your whole heart, and from your whole soul, and from your whole mind, and from your whole strength. This is the first commandment.' But the second is similar to it: 'You shall love your neighbor as yourself.' There is no other commandment greater than these. (Mrk 12:29-31)
Hail Mary…

Beware of the scribes, who prefer to walk in long robes and to be greeted in the marketplace, and to sit in the best seats in the synagogues, and to have the places of honor at feasts, who devour the houses of widows under the pretense of long prayers. These shall receive the more severe judgment. (Mrk 12:38-40)
Hail Mary…

See to it that no one leads you astray. For many will come in my name, saying, 'For I am he,' and they will lead many astray. But when you will have heard of wars and rumors of wars, you should not be afraid. For these things must be, but the end is not so soon. (Mrk 13:5-7)
Hail Mary...

Nation will rise up against nation, and kingdom over kingdom, and there shall be earthquakes in various places, and famines. These are but the beginning of the sorrows. (Mrk 13:8)
Hail Mary…

But see to yourselves. For they will hand you over to councils, and in the synagogues you will be beaten, and you shall stand before governors and kings because of me, as a testimony for them. And the Gospel must first be preached to all nations. (Mrk 13:9-10)
Hail Mary...

Brother will betray brother to death, and the father, a son; and children will rise up against their parents and will bring about their death. And you will be hated by all for the sake of my name. But whoever will have persevered unto the end will be saved. (Mrk 13:12-13)

Hail Mary…

From the fig tree learn its lesson. When its branch becomes tender and puts forth its leaves, you know that summer is very near. So also, when you will have seen these things happen, know that he is very near, at the very gates. (Mrk 13:28-29)
Hail Mary…

This is my blood of the new covenant, which shall be shed for many. Amen I say to you, that I will no longer drink from this fruit of the vine, until that day when I will drink it new in the kingdom of God. (Mrk 14:24-25)
Hail Mary...

Watch and pray, so that you may not enter into temptation. The spirit indeed is willing, but the flesh is weak. (Mrk 14:38)
Hail Mary...

These signs will accompany those who believe. In my name, they shall cast out demons. They will speak in new languages. They will take up serpents, and, if they drink anything deadly, it will not harm them. They shall lay their hands upon the sick, and they will be well. (Mrk 16:17-18)
Hail Mary…

Glory Be…

Words of Jesus (Gospel of Luke)

Our Father...

It is not those who are well who need a physician, but those who are sick. I have not come to call the righteous, but sinners to repentance. (Luk 5:31-32)
Hail Mary...

No one sews a patch from a new garment onto an old garment. Otherwise the new will be torn, and the patch from the new will not match the old. And no one puts new wine into old wineskins. Otherwise, the new wine will burst the wineskins, and it will be poured out, and the wineskins will be destroyed. Instead, the new wine is put into new wineskins, and both are preserved. And no one who is drinking the old, desires new wine, but says, 'The old is good.' (Luk 5:36-39)
Hail Mary...

Love your enemies. Do good to those who hate you. Bless those who curse you, and pray for those who slander you. (Luk 6:27-28)
Hail Mary...

To him who strikes you on the cheek, offer the other also. And from him who takes away your coat, do not withhold even your tunic. (Luk 6:29)
Hail Mary...

Give to everyone who begs from you; and if anyone takes away your goods, do not ask for them again. (Luk 6:30)
Hail Mary...

As you would want others to do to you, do to them also the same. (Luk 6:31)
Hail Mary...

Love your enemies. Do good, and lend, expecting nothing in return. And then your reward will be great, and you will be children of the Most High God, for he himself is kind to the ungrateful and to the wicked. (Luk 6:35)
Hail Mary...

Whoever will be ashamed of me and of my words: of him the Son of man will be ashamed, when he will have arrived in his majesty and that of his Father and of the holy Angels. (Luk 9:26)
Hail Mary...

Whoever will receive this child in my name, receives me; and whoever receives me, receives him who sent me. for the least among all of you is the greatest. (Luk 9:48)
Hail Mary...

No one who puts his hand to the plow, and then looks back, is fit for the kingdom of God. (Luk 9:62)
Hail Mary...

Glory Be...

Decade 2
Our Father...

The harvest is great, but the workers are few. Therefore, ask the Lord of the harvest to send workers into his harvest. (Luk 10:2)
Hail Mary...

Whoever listens to you, listens to me. And whoever rejects you, rejects me. And whoever rejects me, rejects him who sent me. (Luk 10:16)
Hail Mary...

I thank you, Father, Lord of heaven and earth, because you have hidden these things from the wise and the learned, and have revealed them to little ones. Yes, Father, this was how you were pleased to have it happen. (Luk 10:21)
Hail Mary...

Who among you, if he asks his father for bread, he would give him a stone? Or if he asks for a fish, he would give him a serpent, instead of a fish? Or if he will ask for an egg, he would offer to him a scorpion? (Luk 11:11-12)
Hail Mary...

Therefore, if you, being evil, know how to give good things to your children, how much more will your Father give, from heaven, the Holy Spirit to those who ask him? (Luk 11:13)
Hail Mary...

Whoever is not with me is against me, and whoever does not gather with me, scatters. (Luk 11:23)
Hail Mary...

When an unclean spirit has departed from a man, he walks through waterless places, seeking rest. And not finding any, he says: 'I will return to my house, from which I departed.' And when he has arrived, he finds it

swept clean and decorated. Then he goes, and he takes in seven other spirits with him, more wicked than himself, and they enter and live there. And so, the end of that man is made worse than the beginning. (Luk 11:24-26)
Hail Mary…

Do not fear those who kill the body, and afterwards can do nothing more. But I will reveal to you whom you should fear. Fear him who, after he will have killed, has the power to cast into Hell. So I say to you: Fear him. (Luk 12:4-5)
Hail Mary…

Even the very hairs of your head have all been numbered. Therefore, do not be afraid. You are worth more than many sparrows. (Luk 12:7)
Hail Mary…

Watch out and guard yourselves from every kind of greed; for a person's life is not found in the abundance of the things that he possesses. (Luk 12:15)
Hail Mary…

Glory Be…

Decade 3
Our Father…

Sell what you possess, and give alms. Make for yourselves purses that will not wear out, a treasure that will not fall short, in heaven, where no thief approaches, and no moth corrupts. For where your treasure is, there will your heart be also. (Luk 12:33-34)
Hail Mary…

Be dressed for action and have your lamps lit. And let you yourselves be like those waiting for their lord to return from the wedding banquet; so that, when he arrives and knocks, they may open to him promptly. (Luk 12:35)
Hail Mary…

I have come to cast a fire upon the earth. And what should I desire, except that it may be kindled? And I have a baptism, with which to be baptized, and what stress I am under until it is completed! (Luk 12:49-50)
Hail Mary…

Do you think that I have come to give peace to the earth? No, I tell you, but division. For from this time on, there will be five in one house: divided as three against two, and as two against three. (Luk 12:51-52)
Hail Mary…

When you are going with your accuser to the magistrate, while you are on the way, make an effort to settle the case, or he may lead you to the judge, and the judge may deliver you to the officer, and the officer may throw you into prison. I tell you, you will not depart from there, until you have paid the very last penny. (Luk 12:57-58)
Hail Mary…

What is the kingdom of God like, and to what shall I compare it? It is like a grain of mustard seed, which a man took and sowed into his garden. And it grew, and it became a great tree, and the birds of the air made nests in its branches. (Luk 13:18-19)
Hail Mary…

To what shall I compare the kingdom of God? It is like leaven, which a woman took and hid in three measures of fine wheat flour, until it was entirely leavened. (Luk 13:20-21)
Hail Mary…

Strive to enter through the narrow gate. For many, I tell you, will seek to enter and not be able. (Luk 13:24)
Hail Mary...

Some are last who will be first, and some are first who will be last. (Luk 13:30)
Hail Mary…

When you are invited to a wedding, do not sit down in the first place, lest perhaps someone more honored than yourself may have been invited by him. And then he who called both you and him, approaching, may say to you, 'Give this place to him.' And then you would begin, with shame, to take the last place. But when you are invited, go, sit down in the lowest place, so that, when he who invited you arrives, he may say to you, 'Friend, go up higher.' Then you will have glory in the sight of those who sit at the table with you. (Luk 14:8-10)
Hail Mary…

Glory Be…

Decade 4
Our Father…

Everyone who exalts himself shall be humbled, and whoever humbles himself shall be exalted. (Luk 14:11)
Hail Mary...

When you prepare a feast, call the poor, the disabled, the lame, and the blind. And you will be blessed because they do not have a way to repay you. So then, your recompense will be in the resurrection of the just. (Luk 14:13-14)
Hail Mary…

If anyone comes to me, and does not hate his father, and mother, and wife, and children, and brothers, and sisters, and yes, even his own life, he is not able to be my disciple. (Luk 14:26)
Hail Mary...

None of you can become my disciple if you do not give up all your possessions. (Luk 14:33)
Hail Mary...

Who among you, having a hundred sheep, and losing one of them, would not leave the ninety-nine in the desert and go after the one whom he had lost, until he finds it? And when he has found it, he places it on his shoulders, rejoicing. And returning home, he calls together his friends and neighbors, saying to them: 'Rejoice with me! For I have found my sheep, which had been lost.' (Luk 15:4-6)
Hail Mary…

I say to you, that there will be so much more joy in heaven over one sinner repenting, than over the ninety-nine just, who do not need to repent. (Luk 15:7)
Hail Mary…

Rising up, he went to his father. But while he was still at a distance, his father saw him, and he was moved with compassion, and running to him, he fell upon his neck and kissed him. (Luk 15:20)
Hail Mary…

Whoever is faithful in what is least, is also faithful in what is greater. And whoever is dishonest in small matters, is also dishonest in large ones. (Luk 16:10)
Hail Mary...

No servant is able to serve two masters. For either he will hate the one and love the other, or he will be devoted to the one and despise the other. You cannot serve God and wealth. (Luk 16:13)
Hail Mary...

What is prized by men is an abomination in the sight of God. (Luk 16:15)
Hail Mary...

Glory Be…

Decade 5
Our Father…

The law and the prophets were until John came; from that time the kingdom of God is preached, and everyone uses force to enter it. (Luk 16:16)
Hail Mary...

It is easier for heaven and earth to pass away, than for one stroke of a letter in the law to be dropped. (Luk 16:17)
Hail Mary...

Occasions for stumbling are bound to come, but woe to him through whom they come! It would be better for him if a millstone were placed around his neck and he were thrown into the sea, than to lead astray one of these little ones. (Luk 17:1-2)
Hail Mary…

Which of you, having a servant plowing or feeding cattle, would say to him, as he was returning from the field, 'Come in immediately; sit down to eat,' and would not say to him: 'Prepare my dinner; gird yourself and minister to me, while I eat and drink; and after these things, you shall eat and drink?' Would he be grateful to that servant, for doing what he commanded him to do? I think not. So too, when you have done all these things that have been taught to you, you should say: 'We are useless servants. We have done only what we ought to have done.' (Luk 17:7-10)
Hail Mary…

The kingdom of God is not coming with things that can be observed. And so, they will not say, 'Behold, it is here,' or 'Behold, it is there.' For in fact, the kingdom of God is within you. (Luk 17:20-21)
Hail Mary...

Allow the children to come to me, and and do not stop them. for it is to such as these that the kingdom of God belongs. Amen, I say to you, whoever will not accept the kingdom of God like a child, will not enter into it. (Luk 18:16-17)
Hail Mary...

How difficult it is for those who have wealth to enter into the kingdom of God! For it is easier for a camel to pass through the eye of a needle, than for a wealthy man to enter into the kingdom of God. (Luk 18:24-25)
Hail Mary…

So then, I say to you, that to all who have, more will be given. And from him who does not have, even what he has will be taken from him. (Luk 19:26)
Hail Mary...

Be on your guard so that your hearts are not weighed down by self-indulgence and drunkenness and the cares of this life. And then that day may overwhelm you suddenly. For like a snare it will overwhelm all those who sit upon the face of the entire earth. And so, be vigilant, praying at all times, so that you may be held worthy to escape from all these things that will take place, and to stand before the Son of man. (Luk 21:34-36)
Hail Mary...

Whoever is greater among you, let him become as the younger. And whoever is the leader, let him like one who serves. (Luk 22:26)
Hail Mary...

Glory Be...

Words of Jesus (Gospel of John)

Decade 1
Our Father…

Amen, amen, I say to you, unless one has been born from above, he is not able to see the kingdom of God. (Jn 3:3)
Hail Mary…

God so loved the world that he gave his only-begotten Son, so that all who believe in him may not perish, but may have eternal life. (Jn 3:16)
Hail Mary…

Whoever believes in him is not condemned. But whoever does not believe is already condemned, because he does not believe in the name of the only-begotten Son of God. (Jn 3:18)
Hail Mary…

Whoever believes in the Son has eternal life. But whoever is unbelieving toward the Son shall not see life; instead the wrath of God remains upon him. (Jn 3:36)
Hail Mary…

If you knew the gift of God, and who it is who is saying to you, 'Give me to drink,' perhaps you would have made a request of him, and he would have given you living water. (Jn 4:10)
Hail Mary…

All who drink from this water will thirst again. But whoever shall drink from the water that I will give will never be thirsty. The water that I will give will become in them a fountain of water, springing up into eternal life. (Jn 4:13-14)
Hail Mary…

The hour is coming, and it is now, when true worshippers shall worship the Father in spirit and in truth. For the Father seeks such as these to worship him. (Jn 4:23)
Hail Mary…

God is Spirit. And those who worship him must worship in spirit and in truth. (Jn 4:24)
Hail Mary…

Amen, amen, I say to you, that whoever hears my word, and believes in him who sent me, has eternal life, and he does not go into judgment, but instead he crosses from death into life. (Jn 5:24)
Hail Mary...

Amen, I say to you, that the hour is coming, and it is now, when the dead shall hear the voice of the Son of God; and those who hear it shall live. (Jn 5:25)
Hail Mary...

Glory Be...

Decade 2
Our Father...

The hour is coming in which all who are in the grave shall hear the voice of the Son of God. And those who have done good shall go forth to the resurrection of life. Yet truly, those who have done evil shall go to the resurrection of judgment. (Jn 5:28-29)
Hail Mary...

You study the Scriptures for you think that in them you have eternal life. And yet they also offer testimony about me. And you are not willing to come to me, so that you may have life. (Jn 5:39-40)
Hail Mary...

Do not work for food that perishes, but for that which endures to eternal life, which the Son of man will give to you. For it is on him that God the Father has set his seal. (Jn 6:27)
Hail Mary...

This is the work of God, that you believe in him whom he has sent. (Jn 6:29)
Hail Mary...

Amen, amen, I say to you, Moses did not give you bread from heaven, but my Father gives you the true bread from heaven.For the bread of God is he who descends from heaven and gives life to the world. (Jn 6:32-33)
Hail Mary...

I am the bread of life. Whoever comes to me shall not hunger, and whoever believes in me shall never thirst. (Jn 6:35)
Hail Mary...

I descended from heaven, not to do my own will, but the will of him who sent me. Yet this is the will of the Father who sent me: that I should lose

nothing out of all that he has given to me, but that I should raise them up on the last day. (Jn 6:38-39)
Hail Mary…

This is the will of my Father who sent me: that everyone who sees the Son and believes in him may have eternal life, and I will raise him up on the last day. (Jn 6:40)
Hail Mary…

No one is able to come to me, unless the Father, who has sent me, has drawn him. And I will raise him up on the last day. (Jn 6:44)
Hail Mary...

Amen, amen, I say to you, whoever believes in me has eternal life. (Jn 6:47)
Hail Mary…

Glory Be…

Decade 3
Our Father…

I am the bread of life. (Jn 6:48)
Hail Mary…

Your ancestors ate manna in the desert, and they died. This is the bread which descends from heaven, so that if anyone will eat from it, he may not die. (Jn 6:49-50)
Hail Mary…

I am the living bread, who descended from heaven. Whoever eats of this bread will live forever; and the bread that I will give for the life of the world is my flesh. (Jn 6:51)
Hail Mary…

Amen, amen, I say to you, unless you eat the flesh of the Son of man and drink his blood, you will not have life in you. (Jn 6:53)
Hail Mary…

Whoever eats my flesh and drinks my blood has eternal life, and I will raise him up on the last day. For my flesh is true food, and my blood is true drink. (Jn 6:54-55)
Hail Mary…

Whoever eats my flesh and drinks my blood abides in me, and I in him. (Jn 6:56)

Hail Mary…

Just as the living Father has sent me and I live because of the Father, so also whoever eats me will live because of me. (Jn 6:57)
Hail Mary…

This is the bread that descends from heaven. It is not like the manna that your fathers ate, for they died. Whoever eats this bread shall live forever. (Jn 6:58)
Hail Mary…

It is the Spirit who gives life. The flesh is useless. The words that I have spoken to you are spirit and life. (Jn 6:63)
Hail Mary...

If anyone thirsts, let him come to me and drink: whoever believes in me, just as Scripture says, 'Out of the believer's heart shall flow rivers of living water.' Now he said this about the Spirit, which those who believe in him would soon be receiving. (Jn 7:37-39)
Hail Mary…

Glory Be…

Decade 4
Our Father…

I am the light of the world. Whoever follows me does not walk in darkness, but shall have the light of life. (Jn 8:12)
Hail Mary…

If you will abide in my word, you will truly be my disciples. And you shall know the truth, and the truth shall set you free. (Jn 8:31-32)
Hail Mary…

Very truly, I tell you, everyone who commits sin is a slave to sin. The slave does not have a permanent place in the household; the son has a place there forever. So if the Son makes you free, you will be free indeed. (Jn 8:34-36)
Hail Mary…

He said to him, "Do you believe in the Son of God?" He responded and said, "Who is he, Lord, so that I may believe in him?" And Jesus said to him, "You have seen him, and he is the one who is speaking with you." (Jn 9:35-37)
Hail Mary…

Amen, amen, I say to you, he who does not enter through the door into the fold of the sheep, but climbs up by another way, he is a thief and a robber. But he who enters through the door is the shepherd of the sheep. (Jn 10:1-2)
Hail Mary...

I am the gate. Those who enter by me will be saved: and they will come in and go out and will find pastures. (Jn 10:9)
Hail Mary...

The thief comes, so that he may steal and kill and destroy. I have come so that they may have life, and have it more abundantly. (Jn 10:10)
Hail Mary...

I am the good Shepherd. The good Shepherd gives his life for his sheep. (Jn 10:11)
Hail Mary...

I am the good Shepherd, and I know my own, and my own know me. (Jn 10:14)
Hail Mary...

The Father loves me because I lay down my life, so that I may take it back again. No one takes it away from me, but I lay it down voluntarily, For I have power to lay it down: and I have power to take it up again. For I have received this commandment from my Father. (Jn 10:17-18)
Hail Mary...

Glory Be...

Decade 5
Our Father...

My sheep hear my voice. And I know them, and they follow me. And I give them eternal life, and they shall never perish. And no one shall seize them from my hand. (Jn 10:27-28)
Hail Mary...

I am the Resurrection and the Life. Whoever believes in me, even though he has died, he shall live. (Jn 11:25)
Hail Mary...

Amen, amen, I say to you, unless the grain of wheat falls to the ground and dies, it remains just a single grain. But if it dies, it yields much fruit. (Jn 12:24)
Hail Mary...

Whoever loves his life, will lose it. And whoever hates his life in this world, preserves it unto eternal life. (Jn 12:25)
Hail Mary...

Whoever serves me must follow me. And where I am, there will my servant be also. If anyone has served me, my Father will honor him. (Jn 12:26)
Hail Mary...

Now is the judgment of the world. Now will the ruler of this world be cast out. And when I have been lifted up from the earth, I will draw all people to myself. (Jn 12:31-32)
Hail Mary...

For a brief time, the Light is among you. Walk while you have the Light, so that the darkness may not overtake you. But whoever walks in darkness does not know where is he going. While you have the Light, believe in the Light, so that you may be children of Light. (Jn 12:35-36)
Hail Mary...

I have come as a light to the world, so that all who believe in me might not remain in darkness. (Jn 12:46)
Hail Mary...

If anyone has heard my words and not kept them, I do not judge him. For I did not come so that I may judge the world, but so that I may save the world. (Jn 12:47)
Hail Mary...

The one who rejects me and does not receive my word has a judge; on the last day the word that I have spoken will serve as judge. (Jn 12:48)
Hail Mary...

Glory Be...

Jesus and the Father

Decade 1
Our Father…

All things have been handed over to me by my Father. And no one knows the Son except the Father, nor does anyone know the Father except the Son, and those to whom the Son is willing to reveal him. (Matt 11:27)
Hail Mary…

The Father loves the Son, and he has given everything into his hand. (Jn 3:35)
Hail Mary…

My food is to do the will of the One who sent me, so that I may complete his work. (Jn 4:34)
Hail Mary…

My Father is still working, and I also am working. (Jn 5:17)
Hail Mary…

The Jews were seeking to kill him even more so. For not only did he break the Sabbath, but he even said that God was his Father, making himself equal to God. (Jn 5:18)
Hail Mary…

Amen, amen, I say to you, the Son is not able to do anything of himself, but only what he has seen the Father doing. for whatever the Father does, the Son does likewise. (Jn 5:19)
Hail Mary…

The Father loves the Son, and he shows him all that he himself does. And greater works than these will he show him, so much so that you will be astonished. (Jn 5:20)
Hail Mary…

Just as the Father raises the dead and gives life, so also does the Son give life to whomever he wills. (Jn 5:21)
Hail Mary…

The Father does not judge anyone. But he has given all judgment to the Son, so that all may honor the Son, just as they honor the Father. Whoever does not honor the Son, does not honor the Father who sent him. (Jn 5:22-23)

Hail Mary…

Just as the Father has life in himself, so also has he granted to the Son to have life in himself. And he has given him the authority to accomplish judgment. For he is the Son of man. (Jn 5:26-27)
Hail Mary…

Glory Be…

Decade 2
Our Father…

I can do nothing on my own. As I hear, so do I judge. And my judgment is just. For I do not seek my own will, but the will of him who sent me. (Jn 5:30)
Hail Mary…

The works which the Father has given to me to complete, these works themselves that I do, offer testimony about me that the Father has sent me. And the Father who sent me has himself testified on my behalf. (Jn 5:36-37)
Hail Mary…

I have come in the name of my Father, and you do not accept me. If another will come in his own name, you will accept him. How can you believe when you accept glory from one another and do not seek the glory that is from God alone? (Jn 5:43-44)
Hail Mary…

All that the Father gives to me shall come to me. And whoever comes to me, I will not cast out. (Jn 6:37)
Hail Mary…

It has been written in the Prophets: 'And they shall all be taught by God.' Everyone who has listened and learned from the Father comes to me. Not that anyone has seen the Father, except he who is from God; this one has seen the Father. (Jn 6:45-46)
Hail Mary…

My teaching is not of me, but of him who sent me. Anyone who resolves to do the will of God will know whether the teaching is from God or whether I am speaking on my own. Whoever speaks from himself seeks his own glory. But whoever seeks the glory of him who sent him, this one is true, and there is nothing false in him. (Jn 7:16-18)
Hail Mary…

You know me, and you also know where I am from. And I have not come on my own, but he who sent me is true, and you do not know him. I know him because I am from him, and he has sent me. (Jn 7:28-29)
Hail Mary…

You judge according to the flesh. I do not judge anyone. And when I do judge, my judgment is true. For I am not alone, but I and the Father who sent me. (Jn 8:15-16)
Hail Mary…

It is written in your law that the testimony of two men is true. I testify on my own behalf, and the Father who sent me offers testimony about me. (Jn 8:17-18)
Hail Mary…

They said to him, "Where is your Father?" Jesus answered: "You know neither me, nor my Father. If you did know me, perhaps you would know my Father also." (Jn 8:19)
Hail Mary…

Glory Be…

Decade 3
Our Father…

When you will have lifted up the Son of man, then you shall realize that I am he, and that I do nothing of myself, but just as the Father has taught me, so do I speak. (Jn 8:28)
Hail Mary…

He who sent me is with me, and he has not abandoned me alone. For I always do what is pleasing to him. (Jn 8:29)
Hail Mary…

I speak what I have seen with my Father. And you do what you have seen with your father. (Jn 8:38)
Hail Mary…

Jesus said to them: "If God were your father, certainly you would love me. For I proceeded and came from God. For I did not come on my own, but he sent me. (Jn 8:42)
Hail Mary…

If I glorify myself, my glory is nothing. It is my Father who glorifies me. (Jn 8:54)

Hail Mary…

You say about him that he is your God. And yet you have not known him. But I know him. And if I were to say that I do not know him, then I would be like you, a liar. But I know him, and I keep his word. (Jn 8:54-55)
Hail Mary…

I must work the works of him who sent me, while it is day: the night is coming, when no one is able to work. As long as I am in the world, I am the light of the world. (Jn 9:4-5)
Hail Mary…

Just as the Father knows me, and I know the Father. And I lay down my life for my sheep. (Jn 10:15)
Hail Mary…

I and the Father are one. (Jn 10:30)
Hail Mary…

If I do not do the works of my Father, do not believe in me. But if I do them, even if you are not willing to believe in me, believe the works, so that you may know and believe that the Father is in me, and I am in the Father. (Jn 10:37-38)
Hail Mary…

Glory Be…

Decade 4
Our Father…

Whoever believes in me, does not believe in me, but in him who sent me. And whoever sees me, sees him who sent me. (Jn 12:44-45)
Hail Mary…

I am not speaking from myself, but from the Father who sent me. He gave a commandment to me as to what I should say and how I should speak. And I know that his commandment is eternal life. Therefore, the things that I speak, just as the Father has said to me, so also do I speak. (Jn 12:49-50)
Hail Mary…

Before the feast day of the Passover, Jesus knew that the hour was approaching when he would pass from this world to the Father. And since he had always loved his own who were in the world, he loved them unto the end. (Jn 13:1)
Hail Mary…

I am the Way, and the Truth, and the Life. No one comes to the Father, except through me. (Jn 14:6)
Hail Mary…

If you had known me, certainly you would also have known my Father. And from now on, you shall know him, and you have seen him. (Jn 14:7)
Hail Mary…

Philip said to him, "Lord, reveal the Father to us, and it is enough for us." Jesus said to him: "Have I been with you for so long, and you have not known me? Philip, whoever sees me, also sees the Father. How can you say, 'Reveal the Father to us'?" (Jn 14:8-9)
Hail Mary…

Do you not believe that I am in the Father and the Father is in me? The words that I am speaking to you, I do not speak from myself. But the Father abiding in me, he does these works. (Jn 14:10)
Hail Mary…

Do you not believe that I am in the Father and the Father is in me? Or else, believe me because of the works themselves. (Jn 14:11)
Hail Mary…

I do as the Father has commanded me, so that the world may know that I love the Father. (Jn 14:31)
Hail Mary…

Whoever hates me, hates my Father also. (Jn 15:23)
Hail Mary…

Glory Be…

Decade 5
Our Father…

All that the Father has is mine. (Jn 16:15)
Hail Mary…

The Father himself loves you, because you have loved me, and because you have believed that I came from God. I came from the Father, and I have come into the world. Again, I am leaving the world, and I am going to the Father. (Jn 16:27-28)
Hail Mary…

Behold, the hour is coming, and it has now arrived, when you will be scattered, each one on his own, and you will leave me behind, alone. And yet I am not alone, for the Father is with me. (Jn 16:32)
Hail Mary…

Father, the hour has arrived: glorify your Son, so that your Son may glorify you, just as you have given authority over all flesh to him, so that he may give eternal life to all those whom you have given to him.(Jn 17:1-2)
Hail Mary…

I have glorified you on earth. I have completed the work that you gave me to accomplish. And now Father, glorify me within yourself, with the glory that I had with you before the world ever was. (Jn 17:4-5)
Hail Mary…

All that is mine is yours, and all that is yours is mine, and I am glorified in this. (Jn 17:10)
Hail Mary…

Just as you, Father, are in me, and I am in you, so also may they be one in us: so that the world may believe that you have sent me. (Jn 17:21)
Hail Mary…

I am in them, and you are in me. So they may become completely one. And may the world know that you have sent me and that you have loved them, just as you have also loved me. (Jn 17:23)
Hail Mary…

Father, I desire that where I am, those whom you have given to me may also be with me, so that they may see my glory which you have given to me. For you loved me before the foundation of the world. (Jn 17:24)
Hail Mary…

Righteous Father, the world has not known you. But I have known you. And these have known that you sent me. And I have made known your name to them, and I will make it known, so that the love in which you have loved me may be in them, and so that I may be in them. (Jn 17:25-26)
Hail Mary…

Glory Be…

Jesus Commissions the Church

Decade 1
Our Father...

Jesus passed on from there, he saw, sitting at the tax office, a man named Matthew. And he said to him, "Follow me." And rising up, he followed him. (Matt 9:9)
Hail Mary...

The next day again, John was standing with two of his disciples. And catching sight of Jesus walking, he said, "Behold, the Lamb of God." And two disciples were listening to him speaking. And they followed Jesus. (Jn 1:35-37)
Hail Mary...

On the next day, he wanted to go into Galilee, and he found Philip. And Jesus said to him, "Follow me." (Jn 1:43)
Hail Mary...

Passing by the shore of the Sea of Galilee, he saw Simon and his brother Andrew, casting nets into the sea, for they were fishermen. And Jesus said to them, "Come after me, and I will make you fishers of men." And at once abandoning their nets, they followed him. (Mrk 1:16-18)
Hail Mary...

Continuing on a little ways from there, he saw James of Zebedee and his brother John, and they were mending their nets in a boat. And immediately he called them. And leaving behind their father Zebedee in the boat with his hired hands, they followed him. (Mrk 1:19-20)
Hail Mary...

I say to you, that you are Peter, and upon this rock I will build my Church, and the gates of Hell shall not prevail against it. And I will give you the keys of the kingdom of heaven. And whatever you shall bind on earth shall be bound in heaven. And whatever you shall release on earth shall be released, also in heaven. (Matt 16:18-19)
Hail Mary...

Having called together his twelve disciples, he gave them authority over unclean spirits, to cast them out and to cure every sickness and every infirmity. Now the names of the twelve Apostles are these: Simon, who is

called Peter, and Andrew his brother, James of Zebedee, and John his brother, Philip and Bartholomew, Thomas and Matthew the tax collector, and James of Alphaeus, and Thaddaeus, Simon the Canaanite, and Judas Iscariot, who also betrayed him. (Matt 10:1-4)
Hail Mary…

Ascending onto a mountain, he called to himself those whom he willed, and they came to him. (Mrk 3:13)
Hail Mary…

He appointed twelve who would be with him, and so that he might send them out to preach. And he gave them authority to cure the sick, and to cast out demons. (Mrk 3:14-15)
Hail Mary…

Calling together the twelve Apostles, he gave them power and authority over all demons and to cure diseases. And he sent them to preach the kingdom of God and to heal the sick. (Luk 9:1)
Hail Mary…

Glory Be…

Decade 2
Our Father…

He called the twelve. And he began to send them out in twos, and he gave them authority over unclean spirits. (Mrk 6:7)
Hail Mary…

Going out, they were preaching, so that people would repent. And they cast out many demons, and they anointed many of the sick with oil and healed them. (Mrk 6:12-13)
Hail Mary…

Going forth, they traveled around, through the towns, evangelizing and curing everywhere. (Luk 9:6)
Hail Mary…

Jesus sent these twelve, instructing them, saying: "Do not travel by the way of the Gentiles, and do not enter into the city of the Samaritans." (Matt 10:5)
Hail Mary…

But instead go to the sheep who have fallen away from the house of Israel. And going forth, preach, saying: 'For the kingdom of heaven has drawn near.' (Matt 10:6-7)

Hail Mary…

Cure the infirm, raise the dead, cleanse lepers, cast out demons. You have received freely, so give freely. (Matt 10:8)
Hail Mary…

Do not choose to possess gold, nor silver, nor money in your belts, nor provisions for the journey, nor two tunics, nor shoes, nor a staff. For the laborer deserves his portion. (Matt 10:9-10)
Hail Mary…

Into whatever city or town you will enter, inquire as to who is worthy within it. And stay there until you depart. (Matt 10:11)
Hail Mary…

Then, when you enter into the house, greet it, saying, 'Peace to this house.' And if, indeed, that house is worthy, your peace will rest upon it. But if it is not worthy, your peace will return to you. (Matt 10:12-13)
Hail Mary…

Behold, I am sending you like sheep in the midst of wolves. Therefore, be as wise as serpents and as innocent as doves. But beware of men. For they will hand you over to councils, and they will scourge you in their synagogues. (Matt 10:16-17)
Hail Mary…

Glory Be…

Decade 3
Our Father…

You shall be led before both rulers and kings for my sake, as a testimony to them and to the Gentiles. (Matt 10:18)
Hail Mary…

When they hand you over, do not worry about how or what to speak. For what to speak shall be given to you in that hour. For it is not you who will be speaking, but the Spirit of your Father, who will speak through you. (Matt 10:19-20)
Hail Mary…

Go forth to the whole world and preach the Gospel to every creature. Whoever will have believed and been baptized will be saved. Yet truly, whoever will not have believed will be condemned. (Mrk 16:15-16)
Hail Mary…

You are those who have remained with me during my trials. And I confer on you, just as my Father has conferred on me, a kingdom, so that you may eat and drink at my table in my kingdom, and so that you may sit upon thrones, judging the twelve tribes of Israel. (Luk 22:28-30)
Hail Mary...

When I sent you without money or provisions or shoes, did you lack anything? And they said, "Nothing." Then he said to them: "But now, let whoever has money take it, and likewise with provisions. And whoever does not have these, let him sell his coat and buy a sword. (Luk 22:35-36)
Hail Mary...

There will be great earthquakes in various places, and pestilences, and famines, and terrors from heaven; and there will be great signs. But before all these things, they will lay their hands on you and persecute you, handing you over to synagogues and into custody, dragging you before kings and governors, because of my name. And this will be an opportunity for you to give testimony. (Luk 21:11-13)
Hail Mary...

Therefore, set this in your hearts: that you should not consider in advance how you might respond. For I will give to you a mouth and wisdom, which all your adversaries will not be able to resist or contradict. And you will be handed over by your parents, and brothers, and relatives, and friends. And they will bring about the death of some of you. And you will be hated by all because of my name. And yet, not a hair of your head will perish. By your patience, you shall possess your souls. (Luk 21:14-19)
Hail Mary...

Simon, Simon! Behold, Satan has asked for you, so that he may sift you like wheat. But I have prayed for you, so that your faith may not fail, and when once you have turned back, strengthen your brothers. (Luk 22:31-32)
Hail Mary...

He said to them: "You should take nothing for the journey, neither staff, nor traveling bag, nor bread, nor money; and you should not have two tunics. And into whatever house you shall enter, lodge there, and do not move away from there. (Luk 9:3-4)
Hail Mary...

Whoever will not have received you, upon departing from that city, shake off even the dust on your feet, as a testimony against them. (Luk 9:5)
Hail Mary...

Glory Be...

Decade 4

Our Father…

When the Apostles returned, they explained to him all the things that they had done. (Luk 9:10)
Hail Mary…

Whoever listens to you, listens to me. And whoever rejects you, rejects me. And whoever rejects me, rejects him who sent me. (Luk 10:16)
Hail Mary…

Behold, I have given you authority to tread upon serpents and scorpions, and upon all the powers of the enemy, and nothing shall hurt you. (Luk 10:19)
Hail Mary…

All authority has been given to me in heaven and on earth. Therefore, go forth and teach all nations, baptizing them in the name of the Father and of the Son and of the Holy Spirit, teaching them to observe all that I have ever commanded you. And behold, I am with you always, even to the end of the age. (Matt 28:18-20)
Hail Mary…

Amen I say to you, whatever you will have bound on earth, shall be bound also in heaven, and whatever you will have released on earth, shall be released also in heaven. (Matt 18:18)
Hail Mary…

He said to them again: "Peace to you. As the Father has sent me, so I send you." When he had said this, he breathed on them. And he said to them: "Receive the Holy Spirit. Those whose sins you shall forgive, they are forgiven them, and those whose sins you shall retain, they are retained." (Jn 20:21-23)
Hail Mary…

What I tell you in darkness, speak in the light. And what you hear whispered in the ear, preach above the rooftops. (Matt 10:27)
Hail Mary…

Remember my saying that I told you: The servant is not greater than his Lord. If they have persecuted me, they will persecute you also. If they have kept my word, they will keep yours also. But all these things they will do to you because of my name, for they do not know him who sent me. (Jn 15:20-21)
Hail Mary…

When the Advocate has arrived, whom I will send to you from the Father, the Spirit of truth who proceeds from the Father, he will offer testimony about me. And you shall offer testimony, because you are with me from the beginning. (Jn 15:26-27)
Hail Mary…

When they had dined, Jesus said to Simon Peter, "Simon, son of John, do you love me more than these?" He said to him, "Yes, Lord, you know that I love you." He said to him, "Feed my lambs." (Jn 21:15)
Hail Mary…

Glory Be…

Decade 5
Our Father…

He said to him again: "Simon, son of John, do you love me?" He said to him, "Yes, Lord, you know that I love you." He said to him, "Tend my sheep." (Jn 21:16)
Hail Mary…

He said to him a third time, "Simon, son of John, do you love me?" Peter was very grieved that he had asked him a third time, "Do you love me?" And so he said to him: "Lord, you know all things. You know that I love you." He said to him, "Feed my sheep." (Jn 21:17)
Hail Mary…

You will receive power when the Holy Spirit has come upon you, and you shall be witnesses for me in Jerusalem, and in all Judea and Samaria, and even to the ends of the earth. (Acts 1:8)
Hail Mary…

If anyone is in Christ, there is a new creation, everything old has passed away. Behold, all things have been made new. But all is of God, who has reconciled us to himself through Christ, and who has given us the ministry of reconciliation. For certainly God was in Christ, reconciling the world to himself, not charging them with their sins. And he has placed in us the Word of reconciliation. Therefore, we are ambassadors for Christ, so that God is exhorting through us. We beseech you for Christ: be reconciled to God. (2 Cor 5:17-20)
Hail Mary…

Calling in the Apostles, having beaten them, they warned them not to speak at all in the name of Jesus. And they dismissed them. And indeed, they went forth from the presence of the council, rejoicing that they were considered

worthy to suffer insult on behalf of the name of Jesus. And every day, in the temple and among the houses, they did not cease to teach and to evangelize Christ Jesus. (Acts 5:40-42)
Hail Mary…

Philip, descending to a city of Samaria, was preaching Christ to them. And the crowd was listening intently and with one accord to those things which were being said by Philip, and they were watching the signs which he was accomplishing. For many of them had unclean spirits, and, crying out with a loud voice, these departed from them. And many of the paralytics and the lame were cured. Therefore, there was great gladness in that city. (Acts 8:5-9)
Hail Mary…

I dread none of these things. Neither do I consider my life to be more precious because it is my own, provided that in some way I may complete my own course and that of the ministry of the Word, which I received from the Lord Jesus, to testify to the Gospel of the grace of God. (Acts 20:24)
Hail Mary…

Many miracles and signs were accomplished by the Apostles in Jerusalem. And there was a great awe in everyone. And then all who believed were together, and they held all things in common. (Acts 2:43-44)
Hail Mary…

Jesus said to them: "Amen I say to you, that at the resurrection, when the Son of man shall sit on the seat of his majesty, those of you who have followed me shall also sit on twelve seats, judging the twelve tribes of Israel. (Matt 19:28)
Hail Mary…

They went forth, and preached the good news everywhere, the Lord worked with them, and confirmed the word with signs that accompanied it. (Mrk 16:20)
Hail Mary…

Glory Be…

Jesus' Words at the Last Supper

Decade 1
Our Father...

You call me teacher and Lord, and you are right, for that is what I am. Therefore, if I, your Lord and Teacher, have washed your feet, you also ought to wash the feet of one another. For I have given you an example, that you also should do as I have done to you. (Jn 13:13-15)
Hail Mary...

Amen, amen, I say to you, the servant is not greater than his Lord, and the apostle is not greater than he who sent him. If you understand this, you shall be blessed if you will do it. (Jn 13:16-17)
Hail Mary

Amen, amen, I say to you, whoever receives anyone whom I send, receives me. And whoever receives me, receives him who sent me. (Jn 13:20)
Hail Mary...

Now the Son of man has been glorified, and God has been glorified in him. If God has been glorified in him, then God will also glorify him in himself, and he will glorify him without delay. (Jn 13:31-32)
Hail Mary...

I give you a new commandment: Love one another. Just as I have loved you, so also must you love one another. By this, all shall recognize that you are my disciples: if you will have love for one another. (Jn 13:34-35)
Hail Mary...

Do not let your heart be troubled. Believe in God. Believe in me also. (Jn 14:1)
Hail Mary...

In my Father's house, there are many dwelling places. If there were not so, would I have told you that I go to prepare a place for you. And if I go and prepare a place for you, I will return again, and then I will take you to myself, so that where I am, you also may be. (Jn 14:2-3)
Hail Mary...

Amen, amen, I say to you, whoever believes in me shall also do the works that I do. And greater things than these shall he do, for I go to the Father. (Jn 14:12)
Hail Mary...

Whatever you shall ask the Father in my name, that I will do, so that the Father may be glorified in the Son. If you shall ask anything of me in my name, that I will do. (Jn 14:13-14
Hail Mary…

If you love me, you wil keep my commandments. And I will ask the Father, and he will give you another Advocate, so that he may abide with you for eternity: the Spirit of Truth, whom the world cannot receive, because it neither sees him nor knows him. But you shall know him. For he will remain with you, and he will be in you. (Jn 14:15-17)
Hail Mary…

Glory Be…

Decade 2
Our Father…

Whoever holds to my commandments and keeps them: it is he who loves me. And whoever loves me shall be loved by my Father. And I will love him, and I will manifest myself to him. (Jn 14:21)
Hail Mary…

Whoever does not love me, does not keep not my words. And the word that you have heard is not of me, but it is of the Father who sent me. (Jn 14:24)
Hail Mary…

These things I have spoken to you, while abiding with you. But the Advocate, the Holy Spirit, whom the Father will send in my name, will teach you all things and will remind you everything that I have said to you. (Jn 14:25-26)
Hail Mary…

All who love me will keep my word, and my Father will love them, and we will come to them, and will make our home with them. (Jn 14:23)
Hail Mary...

Peace I leave for you; my Peace I give to you. Not in the way that the world gives, do I give to you. Do not let your heart be troubled, and let it not fear. (Jn 14:27)
Hail Mary…

I am the true vine, and my Father is the vinegrower. He removes every branch in me that does not bear fruit. And every branch that does bear fruit, he prunes, so that it may bring forth more fruit. (Jn 15:1-2)
Hail Mary…

Abide in me as I abide in you. Just as the branch is not able to bear fruit of itself, unless it abides in the vine, so also are you unable, unless you abide in me. (Jn 15:4)
Hail Mary…

I am the vine; you are the branches. Whoever abides in me, and I in him, bears much fruit. For without me, you can do nothing. (Jn 15:5)
Hail Mary…

If anyone does not abide in me, he will be thrown away, like a branch, and he will wither; such branches are gathered, cast into the fire, and burned. (Jn 15:6)
Hail Mary…

If you abide in me, and my words abide in you, then you may ask for whatever you will, and it shall be done for you. (Jn 15:7)
Hail Mary…

Glory Be…

Decade 3
Our Father…

In this, my Father is glorified: that you should bear much fruit and become my disciples. (Jn 15:8)
Hail Mary…

As the Father has loved me, so I have loved you. Abide in my love. If you keep my commandments, you shall abide in my love, just as I also have kept my Father's commandments and I abide in his love. (Jn 15:9-10)
Hail Mary…

These things I have spoken to you, so that my joy may be in you, and your joy may be fulfilled. (Jn 15:11)
Hail Mary…

This is my commandment: that you love one another, just as I have loved you. (Jn 15:12)
Hail Mary…

No one has a greater love than this: that he lay down his life for his friends. (Jn 15:13)
Hail Mary…

You are my friends, if you do what I command you. I will no longer call you servants, for the servant does not know what his Lord is doing. But I have called you friends, because everything that I have heard from my Father, I have made known to you. (Jn 15:14-15)
Hail Mary…

You have not chosen me, but I have chosen you. And I have appointed you, so that you may go forth and bear fruit, fruit that will last. Then whatever you have asked of the Father in my name, he will give to you. (Jn 15:16)
Hail Mary…

If the world hates you, know that it has hated me before you. If you had been of the world, the world would love you as its own. Yet truly, you are not of the world, but I have chosen you out of the world; because of this, the world hates you. (Jn 15:18-19)
Hail Mary…

I tell you the truth: it is to your advantage that I am going. For if I do not go, the Advocate will not come to you. But when I will have gone away, I will send him to you. (Jn 16:7)
Hail Mary…

When he comes, he will prove the world wrong about sin and righteousness and judgment: about sin, because they have not believed in me; about righteousness, because I am going to the Father, and you will not see me any longer; about judgment, because the ruler of this world has already been condemned. (Jn 16:8-11)
Hail Mary…

Glory Be…

Decade 4
Our Father…

I still have many things to say to you, but you are not able to bear them now. But when the Spirit of truth has arrived, he will teach the whole truth to you. For he will not be speaking from himself. Instead, whatever he will hear, he will speak. And he will announce to you the things that are to come. (Jn 16:12-13)
Hail Mary…

He shall glorify me. For he will receive from what is mine, and he will announce it to you. All things whatsoever that the Father has are mine. For this reason, I said that he will receive from what is mine and that he will announce it to you. (Jn 16:14-15)
Hail Mary…

Amen, amen, I say to you, that you shall mourn and weep, but the world will rejoice. And you shall be greatly saddened, yet your sorrow shall be turned into joy. (Jn 16:20)
Hail Mary…

A woman, when she is giving birth, has pain, because her hour has arrived. But when she has given birth to the child, then she no longer remembers the difficulties, because of the joy: for a human has been born into the world. Therefore, you also, indeed, have sorrow now. But I will see you again, and your heart shall rejoice. And no one will take away your joy from you. (Jn 16:21-22)
Hail Mary…

Amen, amen, I say to you, if you ask the Father for anything in my name, he will give it to you. Until now, you have not requested anything in my name. Ask, and you shall receive, so that your joy may be full. (Jn 16:23-24)
Hail Mary…

Father, the hour has arrived: glorify your Son, so that your Son may glorify you, just as you have given authority over all flesh to him, so that he may give eternal life to all those whom you have given to him.(Jn 17:1-2)
Hail Mary…

This is eternal life: that they may know you, the only true God, and Jesus Christ, whom you have sent. (Jn 17:3)
Hail Mary…

I have glorified you on earth. I have completed the work that you gave me to accomplish. And now Father, glorify me own presence, with the glory that I had with you before the world ever was. (Jn 17:4-5)
Hail Mary…

I have made your name known to those whom you have given me from the world. They were yours, and you gave them to me. And they have kept your word. Now they realize that all the things that you have given me are from you. (Jn 17:6-7)
Hail Mary…

I have given them the words that you gave to me. And they have kept your words, and they have truly understood that I came from you, and they have believed that you sent me. (Jn 17:8)
Hail Mary…

Glory Be…

Decade 5
Our Father…

Though I am not in the world, these are in the world, and I am coming to you. Father most holy, protect them in your name, those whom you have given to me, so that they may be one, as we are one. (Jn 17:11)
Hail Mary…

While I was with them, I protected them in your name. I have guarded those whom you have given to me, and not one of them is lost, except the one destined to be lost, so that the Scripture may be fulfilled. (Jn 17:12)
Hail Mary…

And now I am coming to you. But I am speaking these things in the world, so that they may have the fullness of my joy within themselves. (Jn 17:13)
Hail Mary…

I have given them your word, and the world has hated them. For they are not of the world, just as I, too, am not of the world. I am not praying that you would take them out of the world, but that you would protect them from evil. They are not of the world, just as I also am not of the world. (Jn 17:14-16)
Hail Mary…

Sanctify them in truth. Your word is truth. (Jn 17:17)
Hail Mary…

Just as you have sent me into the world, I also have sent them into the world. And it is for them that I sanctify myself, so that they also may be sanctified in truth. (Jn 17:18-19)
Hail Mary…

Just as you, Father, are in me, and I am in you, so also may they be one in us: so that the world may believe that you have sent me. (Jn 17:21)
Hail Mary…

The glory that you have given to me, I have given to them, so that they may be one, just as we also are one. (Jn 17:22)

Hail Mary…

Father, I desire that where I am, those whom you have given to me may also be with me, so that they may see my glory which you have given to me. For you loved me before the foundation of the world. (Jn 17:24)
Hail Mary…

I have made known your name to them, and I will make it known, so that the love in which you have loved me may be in them, and so that I may be in them. (Jn 17:26)
Hail Mary…

Glory Be…

Abbreviation

Gen-Genesis
Exo-Exodus
Lev-Leviticus
Num-Numbers
Deut-Deuteronomy
Josh-Joshua
Judg-Judges
Ruth-Ruth
1 Sam-1 Samuel
2 Sam-2 Samuel
1 Kgs-1 Kings
2 Kgs-2 Kings
1 Chron-1 Chronicles
2 Chron-2 Chronicles
Ezr-Ezra
Neh-Nehemiah
Tob-Tobith
Judith-Judith
Est-Esther
1 Mac-1 Maccabees
2 Mac-2 Maccabees
Job-Job
Ps-Psalms
Pro-Proverbs
Eccl-Ecclesiastes

Song-Song of Solomon
Wis-Wisdom
Sir-Sirach
Is- Isaiah
Jer-Jeremiah
Lam-Lamentations
Bar-Baruch
Eze-Ezekiel
Dan-Daniel
Hos-Hosea
Joel-Joel
Amos-Amos
Obad-Obadiah
Jon-Jonah
Mic-Micah
Nah-Nahum
Hab-Habakkuk
Zeph-Zephaniah
Hag-Haggai
Zech-Zechariah
Mal-Malachi
Matt-Matthew
Mrk-Mark
Luk-Luke

Jn-John
Acts-Acts
Rom-Romans
1 Cor-1 Corinthians
2 Cor-2 Corinthians
Gal-Galatians
Eph-Ephesians
Phil-Philippians
Col-Colossians
Tit-Titus
Phlm-Philemon
1 Thes-1 Thessalonians
2 Thes-2 Thessalonians
1 Tim- 1Timothy
2 Tim-2 Timothy
Heb-Hebrew
Jas-James
1 Pet-1 Peter
2 Pet-2 Peter
1 Jn- 1 John
2 Jn- 2 John
3 Jn- 3 John
Jude-Jude
Rev-Revelation

More Titles from Gifted Books and Media

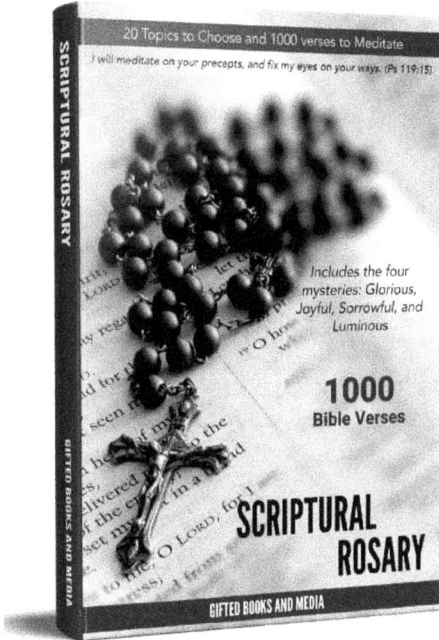

This book is also available as an app on the Appstore

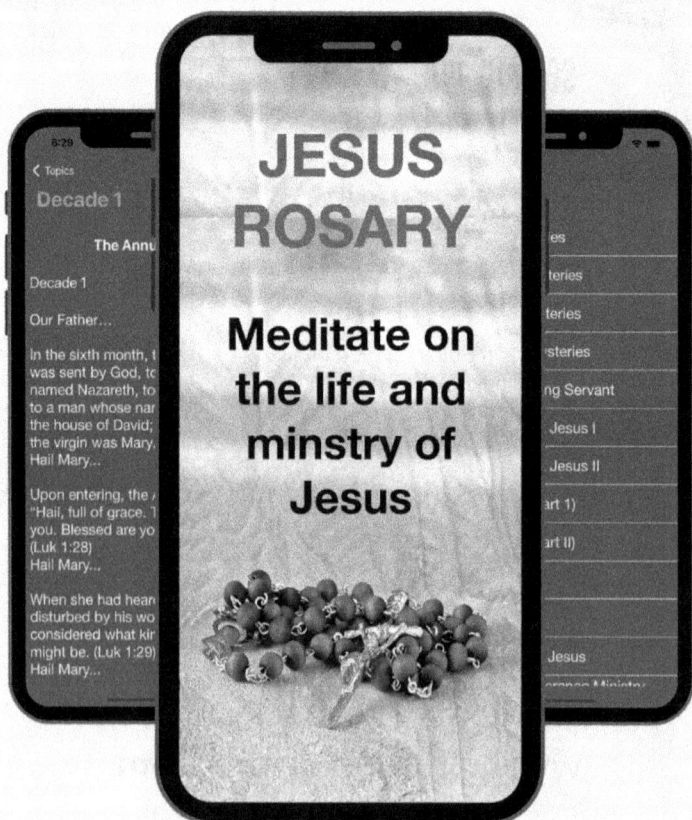

www.ingramcontent.com/pod-product-compliance
Lightning Source LLC
Chambersburg PA
CBHW061728020426
42331CB00006B/1152